PERT Math Practice Workbook

2022

The Most Comprehensive Review for the Math Section of the PERT Test

By

Reza Nazari

Copyright © 2021
Effortless Math Education Inc.

All rights reserved. No part of this publication may be reproduced, stored in a retrieval system, or transmitted in any form or by any means, electronic, mechanical, photocopying, recording, scanning, or otherwise, except as permitted under Section 107 or 108 of the 1976 United States Copyright Ac, without permission of the author.

Effortless Math provides unofficial test prep products for a variety of tests and exams. It is not affiliated with or endorsed by any official organizations.

PERT is a registered trademark of the Postsecondary Education Readiness Test and is not affiliated with Effortless Math.

All inquiries should be addressed to:
info@effortlessMath.com
www.EffortlessMath.com

ISBN: 978-1-63719-026-5

Published by: **Effortless Math Education Inc.**

For Online Math Practice Visit www.EffortlessMath.com

Welcome to
PERT Math Prep 2022

Thank you for choosing Effortless Math for your PERT Math test preparation and congratulations on making the decision to take the PERT test! It's a remarkable move you are taking, one that shouldn't be diminished in any capacity.

That's why you need to use every tool possible to ensure you succeed on the test with the highest possible score, and this extensive math workbook is one such tool.

If math has never been a strong subject for you, don't worry! This book along with our online PERT Math resources will help you prepare for (and even ACE) the PERT Math test. As test day draws nearer, effective preparation becomes increasingly more important. Thankfully, you have this comprehensive workbook to help you get ready for the test. With this book and Effortless Math online resources, you can feel confident that you will be more than ready for the PERT Math test when the time comes.

First and foremost, it is important to note that this book is a workbook and not a textbook. Every lesson of this practice book was carefully developed to ensure that you are making the most effective use of your time while preparing for the test. This up-to-date book reflects the 2022 test guidelines and will put you on the right track to hone your math skills, overcome exam anxiety, and boost your confidence, so that you can have your best to succeed on the PERT Math test.

This exercise book will:

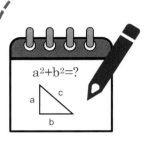

- ☑ Explain the format of the PERT Math test.
- ☑ Describe specific test-taking strategies that you can use on the test.
- ☑ Provide PERT Math test-taking tips.
- ☑ Help you identify the areas in which you need to concentrate your study time.
- ☑ Offer exercises that help you develop the basic math skills you will learn in each section.
- ☑ Give **2 realistic and full-length practice tests** (featuring new question types) with detailed answers to help you measure your exam readiness and build confidence.

This resource contains comprehensive practice questions and exercises that you will need to prepare for the PERT Math test. You'll get numerous skill building exercises as well as tips and techniques on how to prepare for your PERT math test.

In addition, in the following pages you'll find:

➢ **How to Use This Book Effectively** – This section provides you with step-by-step instructions on how to get the most out of this comprehensive study guide.

➢ **How to study for the PERT Math Test** – A six-step study program has been developed to help you make the best use of this book and prepare for your PERT Math test. Here you'll find tips and strategies to guide your study program and help you understand PERT Math and how to ace the test.

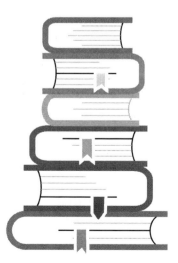

PERT Math Practice Workbook

➢ **PERT Math Review** – Learn everything you need to know about the PERT Math test.

➢ **PERT Math Test-Taking Strategies** – Learn how to effectively put these recommended test-taking techniques into use for improving your PERT Math score.

➢ **Test Day Tips** – Review these tips to make sure you will do your best when the big day comes.

Effortless Math's PERT Online Center

Effortless Math Online PERT Center offers a complete study program, including the following:

- ✓ Step-by-step instructions on how to prepare for the PERT Math test
- ✓ Numerous PERT Math worksheets to help you measure your math skills
- ✓ Complete list of PERT Math formulas
- ✓ Video lessons for all PERT Math topics
- ✓ Full-length PERT Math practice tests
- ✓ And much more…

No Registration Required.

Visit **EffortlessMath.com/PERT** to find your online PERT Math resources.

How to Use This Book Effectively

Look no further when you need a study program to improve your math skills to succeed on the math portion of the PERT test. Each chapter of this comprehensive workbook will provide you with the knowledge, tools, and understanding needed for every topic covered on the test.

It's imperative that you understand each topic before moving onto another one, as that's the way to guarantee your success. You can use Effortless Math online course (a free course) to find examples and a step-by-step guide of every math concept in this workbook to better understand the content that will be on the test. To get the best possible results from this book:

➤ **Begin studying long before your test date.** This provides you ample time to learn the different math concepts. The earlier you begin studying for the test, the sharper your skills will be. Do not procrastinate! Provide yourself with plenty of time to learn the concepts and feel comfortable that you understand them when your test date arrives.

➤ **Practice consistently.** Study PERT Math concepts at least 20 to 30 minutes a day. Remember, slow and steady wins the race, which can be applied to preparing for the PERT Math test. Instead of cramming to tackle everything at once, be patient and learn the math topics in short bursts.

➤ Whenever you get a math problem wrong, **mark it off, and review it later** to make sure you understand the concept.

➤ Start each session by **looking over the previous material.**

➤ Once you've reviewed the book's exercises, **take a practice test at the back of the book** to gauge your level of readiness. Then, review your results. Read detailed answers and solutions for each question you missed.

➤ **Take another practice test** to get an idea of how ready you are to take the actual exam. Taking the practice tests will give you the confidence you need on test day. Simulate the PERT testing environment by sitting in a quiet room free from distraction. Make sure to clock yourself with a timer.

How to Study for the PERT Math Test

Studying for the PERT Math test can be a really daunting and boring task. What's the best way to go about it? Is there a certain study method that works better than others? Well, studying for the PERT Math can be done effectively. The following six-step program has been designed to make preparing for the PERT Math test more efficient and less overwhelming.

Step 1 - Create a study plan
Step 2 - Choose your study resources
Step 3 - Review, Learn, Practice
Step 4 - Learn and practice test-taking strategies
Step 5 - Learn the PERT Test format and take practice tests
Step 6 - Analyze your performance

STEP 1: Create a Study Plan

It's always easier to get things done when you have a plan. Creating a study plan for the PERT Math test can help you to stay on track with your studies. It's important to sit down and prepare a study plan with what works with your life, work, and any other obligations you may have. Devote enough time each day to studying. It's also a great 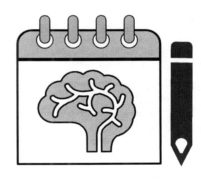 idea to break down each section of the exam into blocks and study one concept at a time.

It's important to understand that there is no "right" way to create a study plan. Your study plan will be personalized based on your specific needs and learning style.

Follow these guidelines to create an effective study plan for your PERT Math test:

★ **Analyze your learning style and study habits** – Everyone has a different learning style. It is essential to embrace your individuality and the unique way you learn. Think about what works and what doesn't work for you. Do you prefer PERT Math prep books or a combination of textbooks and video lessons? Does it work better for you if you study every night for thirty minutes or is it more effective to study in the morning before going to work?

- ★ **Evaluate your schedule** – Review your current schedule and find out how much time you can consistently devote to PERT Math study.

- ★ **Develop a schedule** – Now it's time to add your study schedule to your calendar like any other obligation. Schedule time for study, practice, and review. Plan out which topic you will study on which day to ensure that you're devoting enough time to each concept. Develop a study plan that is mindful, realistic, and flexible.

- ★ **Stick to your schedule** – A study plan is only effective when it is followed consistently. You should try to develop a study plan that you can follow for the length of your study program.

- ★ **Evaluate your study plan and adjust as needed** – Sometimes you need to adjust your plan when you have new commitments. Check in with yourself regularly to make sure that you're not falling behind in your study plan. Remember, the most important thing is sticking to your plan. Your study plan is all about helping you be more productive. If you find that your study plan is not as effective as you want, don't get discouraged. It's okay to make changes as you figure out what works best for you.

STEP 2: Choose Your Study Resources

There are numerous textbooks and online resources available for the PERT Math test, and it may not be clear where to begin. Don't worry! This exercise book reviews all PERT Math concepts and topics. In addition to the book content, you can also use Effortless Math's online resources. (video lessons, worksheets, formulas, etc.) On each page, there is a link (and 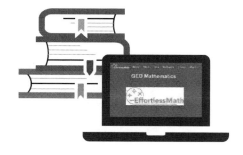 a QR code) to an online webpage which provides a comprehensive review of the topic, step-by-step instruction, video tutorial, and numerous examples and exercises to help you fully understand the concept.

Simply visit EffortlessMath.com/PERT to find your online PERT Math resources.

STEP 3: Review, Learn, Practice

This PERT Math exercise book breaks down each subject into specific skills or content areas. For instance, the percent concept is separated into different topics–percent calculation, percent increase and decrease, percent problems, etc. Use this book to help you go over all key math concepts and topics on the PERT Math test.

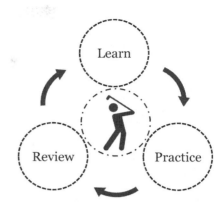

As you review each topic, take notes or highlight the concepts you would like to go over again in the future. If you're unfamiliar with a topic or something is difficult for you, use the link (or the QR code) at the top of the page to find the webpage that provides more instruction about that topic. For each math topic, plenty of instructions, step-by-step guides, and examples are provided to ensure you get a good grasp of the material.

Quickly review the topics you do understand to get a brush-up of the material. Be sure to do the practice questions provided at the end of every chapter to measure your understanding of the concepts.

STEP 4: Learn and Practice Test-taking Strategies

In the following sections, you will find important test-taking strategies and tips that can help you earn extra points. You'll learn how to think strategically and when to guess if you don't know the answer to a question. Using PERT Math test-taking strategies and tips can help you raise your score and do well on the test. Apply test taking strategies on the practice tests to help you boost your confidence.

STEP 5: Learn the PERT Test Format and Take Practice Tests

The *PERT Test Review* section provides information about the structure of the PERT test. Read this section to learn more about the PERT test structure, different test sections, the number of questions in each section, and the section time limits. When you have a prior understanding of the test format and different types of PERT Math questions, you'll feel more confident when you take the actual exam.

Once you have read through the instructions and lessons and feel like you are ready to go – take advantage of both of the full-length PERT Math practice tests available in this exercise book. Use the practice tests to sharpen your skills and build confidence.

The PERT Math practice tests offered at the end of the book are formatted similarly to the actual PERT Math test. When you take each practice test, try to simulate actual testing conditions. To take the practice tests, sit in a quiet space, time yourself, and work through as many of the questions as time allows. The practice tests are followed by detailed answer explanations to help you find your weak areas, learn from your mistakes, and raise your PERT Math score.

STEP 6: Analyze Your Performance

After taking the practice tests, look over the answer keys and explanations to learn which questions you answered correctly and which you did not. Never be discouraged if you make a few mistakes. See them as a learning opportunity. This will highlight your strengths and weaknesses.

You can use the results to determine if you need additional practice or if you are ready to take the actual PERT Math test.

Looking for more?

Visit EffortlessMath.com/PERT to find hundreds of PERT Math worksheets, video tutorials, practice tests, PERT Math formulas, and much more.

Or scan this QR code.

No Registration Required.

PERT Test Review

The Postsecondary Education Readiness Test, is known as the PERT, is a test to determine the appropriate level of college course work for an incoming student. In essence, it is a broad and quick assessment of students' academic abilities.

The PERT test consists of three multiple-choice separate exams:

- Mathematics
- Reading
- Writing

The PERT test is a Computer Adaptive Test (CAT). It means that if the correct answer is chosen, the next question will be harder. If the answer given is incorrect, the next question will be easier. This also means that once an answer is selected on the CAT it cannot be changed.

The mathematics portion of the PERT test contains 30 multiple-choice questions. The test covers data analysis, geometry, and algebra on both intermediate and basic levels. The topics on the math test includes:

- linear equations, linear inequalities, literal equation, and quadratic formulas
- simultaneous linear equations with two variables
- evaluating algebraic expressions
- translating between lines and inspecting equations on coordinate planes
- dividing by binomials and monomials
- adding, subtracting, multiplying, dividing, simplifying and factoring polynomial

Students are not allowed to use calculator when taking a PERT assessment. A pop-up calculator is embedded in the test for some questions. Scores on the PERT test range from 50 to 150. On the PERT mathematics exam, you will be placed in lower-level developmental education if you score between 50-95. If your score is between 96 and 113, then you will be placed in higher level developmental education. A score of 114 to 122 will enable you to be place in Intermediate Algebra (MAT 1033). Score of 123 or higher will allow you to take College Algebra or higher (MAC 1105).

PERT Math Test-Taking Strategies

Here are some test-taking strategies that you can use to maximize your performance and results on the PERT Math test.

#1: USE THIS APPROACH TO ANSWER EVERY PERT MATH QUESTION

- Review the question to identify keywords and important information.
- Translate the keywords into math operations so you can solve the problem.
- Review the answer choices. What are the differences between answer choices?
- Draw or label a diagram if needed.
- Try to find patterns.
- Find the right method to answer the question. Use straightforward math, plug in numbers, or test the answer choices (backsolving).
- Double-check your work.

#2: USE EDUCATED GUESSING

This approach is applicable to the problems you understand to some degree but cannot solve using straightforward math. In such cases, try to filter out as many answer choices as possible before picking an answer. In cases where you don't have a clue about what a certain problem entails, don't waste any time trying to eliminate answer choices. Just choose one randomly before moving onto the next question.

As you can ascertain, direct solutions are the most optimal approach. Carefully read through the question, determine what the solution is using the math you have learned before, then coordinate the answer with one of the choices available to you. Are you stumped? Make your best guess, then move on.

Don't leave any fields empty! Even if you're unable to work out a problem, strive to answer it. Take a guess if you have to. You will not lose points by getting an answer wrong, though you may gain a point by getting it correct!

#3: BALLPARK

A ballpark answer is a rough approximation. When we become overwhelmed by calculations and figures, we end up making silly mistakes. A decimal that is moved by one unit can change an answer from right to wrong, regardless of the number of steps that you went through to get it. That's where ballparking can play a big part.

If you think you know what the correct answer may be (even if it's just a ballpark answer), you'll usually have the ability to eliminate a couple of choices. While answer choices are usually based on the average student error and/or values that are closely tied, you will still be able to weed out choices that are way far afield. Try to find answers that aren't in the proverbial ballpark when you're looking for a wrong answer on a multiple-choice question. This is an optimal approach to eliminating answers to a problem.

#4: BACKSOLVING

A majority of questions on the PERT Math test will be in multiple-choice format. Many test-takers prefer multiple-choice questions, as at least the answer is right there. You'll typically have four answers to pick from. You simply need to figure out which one is correct. Usually, the best way to go about doing so is "backsolving."

As mentioned earlier, direct solutions are the most optimal approach to answering a question. Carefully read through a problem, calculate a solution, then correspond the answer with one of the choices displayed in front of you. If you can't calculate a solution, your next best approach involves "backsolving."

When backsolving a problem, contrast one of your answer options against the problem you are asked, then see which of them is most relevant. More often than not, answer choices are listed in ascending or descending order. In such cases, try out the choices B or C. If it's not correct, you can go either down or up from there.

#5 : PLUGGING IN NUMBERS

"Plugging in numbers" is a strategy that can be applied to a wide range of different math problems on the PERT Math test. This approach is typically used to simplify a challenging question so that it is more understandable. By using the strategy carefully, you can find the answer without too much trouble.

The concept is fairly straightforward—replace unknown variables in a problem with certain values. When selecting a number, consider the following:

- Choose a number that's basic (just not too basic). Generally, you should avoid choosing 1 (or even 0). A decent choice is 2.

- Try not to choose a number that is displayed in the problem.

- Make sure you keep your numbers different if you need to choose at least two of them.

- More often than not, choosing numbers merely lets you filter out some of your answer choices. As such, don't just go with the first choice that gives you the right answer.

- If several answers seem correct, then you'll need to choose another value and try again. This time, though, you'll just need to check choices that haven't been eliminated yet.

- If your question contains fractions, then a potential right answer may involve either an LCD (least common denominator) or an LCD multiple.

- 100 is the number you should choose when you are dealing with problems involving percentages.

PERT Math – Test Day Tips

After practicing and reviewing all the math concepts you've been taught, and taking some PERT mathematics practice tests, you'll be prepared for test day. Consider the following tips to be extra-ready come test time.

Before Your Test

What to do the night before:

- **Relax!** One day before your test, study lightly or skip studying altogether. You shouldn't attempt to learn something new, either. There are plenty of reasons why studying the evening before a big test can work against you. Put it this way–a marathoner wouldn't go out for a sprint before the day of a big race. Mental marathoners–such as yourself–should not study for any more than one hour 24 hours before a PERT test. That's because your brain requires some rest to be at its best. The night before your exam, spend some time with family or friends, or read a book.

- **Avoid bright screens** - You'll have to get some good shuteye the night before your test. Bright screens (such as the ones coming from your laptop, TV, or mobile device) should be avoided altogether. Staring at such a screen will keep your brain up, making it hard to drift asleep at a reasonable hour.

- **Make sure your dinner is healthy** - The meal that you have for dinner should be nutritious. Be sure to drink plenty of water as well. Load up on your complex carbohydrates, much like a marathon runner would do. Pasta, rice, and potatoes are ideal options here, as are vegetables and protein sources.

- **Get your bag ready for test day** - The night prior to your test, pack your bag with your stationery, admissions pass, ID, and any other gear that you need. Keep the bag right by your front door.

- **Make plans to reach the testing site** - Before going to sleep, ensure that you understand precisely how you will arrive at the site of the test. If parking is something you'll have to find first, plan for it. If you're dependent on public transit, then review the schedule. You should also make sure that the train/bus/subway/streetcar you use will be running. Find out about road closures as well. If a parent or friend is accompanying you, ensure that they understand what steps they have to take as well.

The Day of the Test

- **Get up reasonably early, but not too early.**

- **Have breakfast** - Breakfast improves your concentration, memory, and mood. As such, make sure the breakfast that you eat in the morning is healthy. The last thing you want to be is distracted by a grumbling tummy. If it's not your own stomach making those noises, another test taker close to you might be instead. Prevent discomfort or embarrassment by consuming a healthy breakfast. Bring a snack with you if you think you'll need it.

- **Follow your daily routine** - Do you watch Good Morning America each morning while getting ready for the day? Don't break your usual habits on the day of the test. Likewise, if coffee isn't something you drink in the morning, then don't take up the habit hours before your test. Routine consistency lets you concentrate on the main objective—doing the best you can on your test.

- **Wear layers** - Dress yourself up in comfortable layers. You should be ready for any kind of internal temperature. If it gets too warm during the test, take a layer off.

- **Get there on time** - The last thing you want to do is get to the test site late. Rather, you should be there 45 minutes prior to the start of the test. Upon your arrival, try not to hang out with anybody who is nervous. Any anxious energy they exhibit shouldn't influence you.

- **Leave the books at home** - No books should be brought to the test site. If you start developing anxiety before the test, books could encourage you to do some last-minute studying, which will only hinder you. Keep the books far away—better yet, leave them at home.

- **Make your voice heard** - If something is off, speak to a proctor. If medical attention is needed or if you'll require anything, consult the proctor prior to the start of the test. Any doubts you have should be clarified. You should be entering the test site with a state of mind that is completely clear.

- **Have faith in yourself** - When you feel confident, you will be able to perform at your best. When you are waiting for the test to begin, envision yourself receiving an outstanding result. Try to see yourself as someone who knows all the answers, no matter what the questions are. A lot of athletes tend to use this technique–particularly before a big competition. Your expectations will be reflected by your performance.

During your test

- **Be calm and breathe deeply** - You need to relax before the test, and some deep breathing will go a long way to help you do that. Be confident and calm. You got this. Everybody feels a little stressed out just before an evaluation of any kind is set to begin. Learn some effective breathing exercises. Spend a minute meditating before the test starts. Filter out any negative thoughts you have. Exhibit confidence when having such thoughts.

- **Concentrate on the test** - Refrain from comparing yourself to anyone else. You shouldn't be distracted by the people near you or random noise. Concentrate exclusively on the test. If you find yourself irritated by surrounding noises, earplugs can be used to block sounds off close to you. Don't forget–the test is going to last several hours if you're taking more than one subject of the test. Some of that time will be dedicated to brief sections. Concentrate on the specific section you are working on during a particular moment. Do not let your mind wander off to upcoming or previous sections.

- **Try to answer each question individually** - Focus only on the question you are working on. Use one of the test-taking strategies to solve the problem. If you aren't able to come up with an answer, don't get frustrated. Simply skip that question, then move onto the next one.

- **Don't forget to breathe!** Whenever you notice your mind wandering, your stress levels boosting, or frustration brewing, take a thirty-second break. Shut your eyes, drop your pencil, breathe deeply, and let your shoulders relax. You will end up being more productive when you allow yourself to relax for a moment.

- **Optimize your breaks** - When break time comes, use the restroom, have a snack, and reactivate your energy for the subsequent section. Doing some stretches can help stimulate your blood flow.

After your test

- **Take it easy** - You will need to set some time aside to relax and decompress once the test has concluded. There is no need to stress yourself out about what you could've said, or what you may have done wrong. At this point, there's nothing you can do about it. Your energy and time would be better spent on something that will bring you happiness for the remainder of your day.

- **Redoing the test** - Did you pass the test? Congratulations! Your hard work paid off!

If you have failed your test, though, don't worry! The test can be retaken. In such cases, you will need to follow the retake policy. You also need to re-register to take the exam again.

Contents

Chapter 1: Fractions and Mixed Numbers 1
- Simplifying Fractions 2
- Adding and Subtracting Fractions 3
- Multiplying and Dividing Fractions 4
- Adding Mixed Numbers 5
- Subtracting Mixed Numbers 6
- Multiplying Mixed Numbers 7
- Dividing Mixed Numbers 8
- Answers – Chapter 1 9

Chapter 2: Decimal 13
- Comparing Decimals 14
- Rounding Decimals 15
- Adding and Subtracting Decimals 16
- Multiplying and Dividing Decimals 17
- Answers – Chapter 2 18

Chapter 3: Integers and Order of Operations 21
- Adding and Subtracting Integers 22
- Multiplying and Dividing Integers 23
- Order of Operation 24
- Integers and Absolute Value 25
- Answers – Chapter 3 26

Chapter 4: Ratios and Proportions 29
- Simplifying Ratios 30
- Proportional Ratios 31
- Create Proportion 32
- Similarity and Ratios 33
- Simple Interest 34
- Answers – Chapter 4 35

Contents

Chapter 5: Percentage 39
Percent Problems 40
Percent of Increase and Decrease 41
Discount, Tax and Tip 42
Answers – Chapter 5 43

Chapter 6: Expressions and Variables 45
Simplifying Variable Expressions 46
Simplifying Polynomial Expressions 47
Evaluating One Variable 48
Evaluating Two Variables 49
The Distributive Property 50
Answers – Chapter 6 51

Chapter 7: Equations and Inequalities 55
One–Step Equations 56
Multi –Step Equations 57
System of Equations 58
Graphing Single–Variable Inequalities 59
One–Step Inequalities 60
Multi –Step Inequalities 61
Answers – Chapter 7 62

Chapter 8: Lines and Slope 67
Finding Slope 68
Graphing Lines Using Slope–Intercept Form 69
Writing Linear Equations 70
Finding Midpoint 71
Finding Distance of Two Points 72
Answers – Chapter 8 73

Chapter 9: Exponents and Variables 77
Multiplication Property of Exponents 78
Division Property of Exponents 79
Powers of Products and Quotients 80
Zero and Negative Exponents 81
Negative Exponents and Negative Bases 82
Scientific Notation 83
Radicals 84
Answers – Chapter 9 85

Chapter 10: Polynomials 91
Simplifying Polynomials 92
Adding and Subtracting Polynomials 93
Multiplying Monomials 94
Multiplying and Dividing Monomials 95
Multiplying a Polynomial and a Monomial 96
Multiplying Binomials 97
Factoring Trinomials 98
Answers – Chapter 10 99

Chapter 11: Geometry and Solid Figures 105
The Pythagorean Theorem 106
Triangles 107
Polygons 108
Circles 109
Cubes 110
Trapezoids 111
Rectangular Prisms 112
Cylinder 113
Answers – Chapter 11 114

Contents

Chapter 12: Statistics 117
- Mean, Median, Mode, and Range of the Given Data 118
- Pie Graph 119
- Probability Problems 120
- Permutations and Combinations 121
- Answers – Chapter 12 122

Chapter 13: Functions Operations 125
- Function Notation and Evaluation 126
- Adding and Subtracting Functions 127
- Multiplying and Dividing Functions 128
- Composition of Functions 129
- Answers – Chapter 13 130

Time to Test 132

PERT Mathematics Practice Test 1 133

PERT Mathematics Practice Test 2 143

PERT Math Practice Tests Answer Keys 153

PERT Mathematics Practice Tests Answers and Explanations 155

Chapter 1: Fractions and Mixed Numbers

Math Topics that you'll learn in this Chapter:

- ✓ Simplifying Fractions
- ✓ Adding and Subtracting Fractions
- ✓ Multiplying and Dividing Fractions
- ✓ Adding Mixed Numbers
- ✓ Subtracting Mixed Numbers
- ✓ Multiplying Mixed Numbers
- ✓ Dividing Mixed Numbers

Chapter 1: Fractions and Mixed Numbers

Simplifying Fractions

✎ *Simplify each fraction.*

1) $\frac{8}{16} =$

2) $\frac{7}{21} =$

3) $\frac{11}{44} =$

4) $\frac{6}{24} =$

5) $\frac{6}{18} =$

6) $\frac{18}{27} =$

7) $\frac{15}{55} =$

8) $\frac{24}{54} =$

9) $\frac{63}{72} =$

10) $\frac{40}{64} =$

11) $\frac{23}{46} =$

12) $\frac{35}{63} =$

13) $\frac{32}{36} =$

14) $\frac{81}{99} =$

15) $\frac{16}{64} =$

16) $\frac{14}{35} =$

17) $\frac{19}{38} =$

18) $\frac{18}{54} =$

19) $\frac{56}{70} =$

20) $\frac{40}{45} =$

21) $\frac{9}{90} =$

22) $\frac{20}{25} =$

23) $\frac{36}{42} =$

24) $\frac{40}{48} =$

25) $\frac{18}{54} =$

26) $\frac{48}{144} =$

Chapter 1: Fractions and Mixed Numbers

Adding and Subtracting Fractions

✎ *Calculate and write the answer in lowest term.*

1) $\dfrac{1}{3} + \dfrac{1}{5} =$

2) $\dfrac{2}{5} + \dfrac{3}{8} =$

3) $\dfrac{1}{3} - \dfrac{2}{9} =$

4) $\dfrac{4}{5} - \dfrac{2}{9} =$

5) $\dfrac{2}{9} + \dfrac{1}{3} =$

6) $\dfrac{3}{10} + \dfrac{2}{5} =$

7) $\dfrac{9}{10} - \dfrac{4}{5} =$

8) $\dfrac{7}{9} - \dfrac{3}{7} =$

9) $\dfrac{3}{4} + \dfrac{1}{3} =$

10) $\dfrac{3}{8} + \dfrac{2}{5} =$

11) $\dfrac{3}{4} - \dfrac{2}{5} =$

12) $\dfrac{7}{9} - \dfrac{2}{3} =$

13) $\dfrac{4}{9} + \dfrac{5}{6} =$

14) $\dfrac{2}{3} + \dfrac{1}{4} =$

15) $\dfrac{9}{10} - \dfrac{3}{5} =$

16) $\dfrac{7}{12} - \dfrac{1}{2} =$

17) $\dfrac{4}{5} + \dfrac{2}{3} =$

18) $\dfrac{5}{7} + \dfrac{1}{5} =$

19) $\dfrac{5}{9} - \dfrac{2}{5} =$

20) $\dfrac{3}{5} - \dfrac{2}{9} =$

21) $\dfrac{7}{9} + \dfrac{1}{7} =$

22) $\dfrac{5}{8} + \dfrac{2}{3} =$

23) $\dfrac{5}{7} - \dfrac{2}{5} =$

24) $\dfrac{7}{9} - \dfrac{3}{4} =$

25) $\dfrac{3}{5} - \dfrac{1}{6} =$

26) $\dfrac{3}{12} + \dfrac{2}{7} =$

Chapter 1: Fractions and Mixed Numbers

Multiplying and Dividing Fractions

✎ Solve and write the answer in lowest term.

1) $\frac{1}{3} \times \frac{9}{5} =$

2) $\frac{1}{4} \times \frac{3}{7} =$

3) $\frac{1}{5} \div \frac{1}{4} =$

4) $\frac{1}{6} \div \frac{5}{12} =$

5) $\frac{2}{3} \times \frac{4}{7} =$

6) $\frac{5}{7} \times \frac{3}{4} =$

7) $\frac{2}{5} \div \frac{3}{7} =$

8) $\frac{3}{7} \div \frac{5}{8} =$

9) $\frac{3}{8} \times \frac{4}{7} =$

10) $\frac{2}{9} \times \frac{6}{11} =$

11) $\frac{1}{10} \div \frac{3}{8} =$

12) $\frac{3}{10} \div \frac{4}{5} =$

13) $\frac{6}{7} \times \frac{4}{9} =$

14) $\frac{3}{7} \times \frac{5}{6} =$

15) $\frac{7}{9} \div \frac{6}{11} =$

16) $\frac{1}{15} \div \frac{2}{3} =$

17) $\frac{1}{13} \times \frac{1}{2} =$

18) $\frac{1}{12} \times \frac{4}{7} =$

19) $\frac{1}{15} \div \frac{4}{9} =$

20) $\frac{1}{16} \div \frac{1}{2} =$

21) $\frac{4}{7} \times \frac{5}{8} =$

22) $\frac{1}{11} \times \frac{4}{5} =$

23) $\frac{1}{16} \div \frac{5}{8} =$

24) $\frac{1}{15} \div \frac{2}{3} =$

25) $\frac{1}{13} \times \frac{2}{5} =$

26) $\frac{1}{18} \times \frac{3}{7} =$

Chapter 1: Fractions and Mixed Numbers

Adding Mixed Numbers

✍ *Solve and write the answer in lowest terms.*

1) $1\frac{1}{5} + 2\frac{2}{5} =$

2) $1\frac{1}{2} + 4\frac{5}{6} =$

3) $2\frac{4}{5} + 2\frac{3}{10} =$

4) $3\frac{1}{6} + 2\frac{2}{5} =$

5) $1\frac{5}{6} + 1\frac{2}{5} =$

6) $3\frac{5}{7} + 1\frac{2}{9} =$

7) $3\frac{5}{8} + 2\frac{1}{3} =$

8) $1\frac{6}{7} + 3\frac{2}{9} =$

9) $2\frac{5}{9} + 1\frac{1}{4} =$

10) $3\frac{7}{9} + 2\frac{5}{6} =$

11) $2\frac{1}{10} + 2\frac{2}{5} =$

12) $1\frac{3}{10} + 3\frac{4}{5} =$

13) $3\frac{1}{12} + 2\frac{1}{3} =$

14) $5\frac{1}{11} + 1\frac{1}{2} =$

15) $3\frac{1}{21} + 2\frac{2}{3} =$

16) $4\frac{1}{24} + 1\frac{5}{8} =$

17) $2\frac{1}{25} + 3\frac{3}{5} =$

18) $3\frac{1}{15} + 2\frac{2}{10} =$

19) $5\frac{6}{7} + 2\frac{1}{3} =$

20) $2\frac{1}{8} + 3\frac{3}{4} =$

21) $2\frac{5}{7} + 2\frac{2}{21} =$

22) $4\frac{1}{6} + 1\frac{4}{5} =$

23) $2\frac{1}{7} + 2\frac{3}{8} =$

24) $3\frac{1}{4} + 2\frac{2}{3} =$

25) $1\frac{1}{13} + 2\frac{3}{4} =$

26) $3\frac{2}{35} + 2\frac{5}{7} =$

Chapter 1: Fractions and Mixed Numbers

Subtracting Mixed Numbers

✎ *Solve and write the answer in lowest terms.*

1) $5\frac{2}{9} - 2\frac{1}{9} =$

2) $6\frac{2}{7} - 2\frac{1}{3} =$

3) $5\frac{3}{8} - 2\frac{3}{4} =$

4) $7\frac{2}{5} - 3\frac{1}{10} =$

5) $9\frac{5}{7} - 7\frac{4}{21} =$

6) $11\frac{7}{12} - 9\frac{5}{6} =$

7) $9\frac{5}{9} - 8\frac{1}{8} =$

8) $13\frac{7}{9} - 11\frac{3}{7} =$

9) $8\frac{7}{12} - 7\frac{3}{8} =$

10) $11\frac{5}{9} - 9\frac{1}{4} =$

11) $6\frac{5}{6} - 2\frac{2}{9} =$

12) $5\frac{7}{8} - 4\frac{1}{3} =$

13) $9\frac{5}{8} - 8\frac{1}{2} =$

14) $4\frac{9}{16} - 2\frac{1}{4} =$

15) $3\frac{2}{3} - 1\frac{2}{15} =$

16) $5\frac{1}{2} - 4\frac{2}{17} =$

17) $5\frac{6}{7} - 2\frac{1}{3} =$

18) $3\frac{3}{7} - 2\frac{2}{21} =$

19) $7\frac{3}{10} - 5\frac{2}{15} =$

20) $4\frac{5}{6} - 2\frac{2}{9} =$

21) $6\frac{3}{7} - 2\frac{2}{9} =$

22) $7\frac{4}{5} - 6\frac{3}{7} =$

23) $12\frac{3}{7} - 8\frac{1}{3} =$

24) $5\frac{4}{9} - 2\frac{5}{6} =$

25) $10\frac{1}{28} - 7\frac{3}{4} =$

26) $11\frac{5}{12} - 7\frac{5}{48} =$

Chapter 1: Fractions and Mixed Numbers

Multiplying Mixed Numbers

✎ *Solve and write the answer in lowest terms.*

1) $1\frac{1}{6} \times 1\frac{3}{7} =$

2) $5\frac{1}{6} \times 2\frac{1}{4} =$

3) $3\frac{3}{7} \times 1\frac{2}{9} =$

4) $3\frac{3}{8} \times 3\frac{1}{6} =$

5) $1\frac{1}{2} \times 5\frac{2}{3} =$

6) $3\frac{1}{2} \times 6\frac{2}{3} =$

7) $9\frac{1}{2} \times 2\frac{1}{6} =$

8) $2\frac{5}{8} \times 8\frac{3}{5} =$

9) $3\frac{4}{5} \times 4\frac{2}{3} =$

10) $5\frac{1}{3} \times 2\frac{2}{7} =$

11) $6\frac{1}{3} \times 3\frac{3}{4} =$

12) $7\frac{2}{3} \times 1\frac{8}{9} =$

13) $8\frac{1}{2} \times 2\frac{1}{6} =$

14) $4\frac{1}{5} \times 8\frac{2}{3} =$

15) $3\frac{1}{8} \times 5\frac{2}{3} =$

16) $2\frac{2}{7} \times 6\frac{2}{5} =$

17) $2\frac{3}{8} \times 7\frac{2}{3} =$

18) $1\frac{7}{8} \times 8\frac{2}{3} =$

19) $9\frac{1}{2} \times 3\frac{1}{5} =$

20) $2\frac{5}{8} \times 4\frac{1}{3} =$

21) $6\frac{1}{3} \times 3\frac{2}{5} =$

22) $5\frac{3}{4} \times 2\frac{2}{7} =$

23) $8\frac{1}{6} \times 2\frac{2}{7} =$

24) $4\frac{1}{6} \times 7\frac{1}{5} =$

25) $2\frac{1}{5} \times 2\frac{5}{8} =$

26) $6\frac{2}{3} \times 4\frac{3}{5} =$

Chapter 1: Fractions and Mixed Numbers

Dividing Mixed Numbers

✎ **Solve and write the answer in lowest terms.**

1) $6\frac{1}{2} \div 4\frac{2}{5} =$

2) $1\frac{3}{8} \div 1\frac{1}{4} =$

3) $6\frac{2}{5} \div 2\frac{4}{5} =$

4) $7\frac{1}{3} \div 6\frac{3}{4} =$

5) $7\frac{2}{5} \div 3\frac{3}{4} =$

6) $2\frac{4}{5} \div 3\frac{2}{3} =$

7) $8\frac{3}{5} \div 4\frac{3}{4} =$

8) $6\frac{3}{4} \div 2\frac{2}{9} =$

9) $5\frac{2}{7} \div 2\frac{2}{9} =$

10) $2\frac{2}{5} \div 3\frac{3}{5} =$

11) $4\frac{3}{7} \div 1\frac{7}{8} =$

12) $2\frac{5}{7} \div 2\frac{4}{5} =$

13) $8\frac{3}{5} \div 6\frac{1}{5} =$

14) $2\frac{5}{8} \div 1\frac{8}{9} =$

15) $5\frac{6}{7} \div 2\frac{3}{4} =$

16) $1\frac{3}{5} \div 2\frac{3}{8} =$

17) $5\frac{3}{4} \div 3\frac{2}{5} =$

18) $2\frac{3}{4} \div 3\frac{1}{5} =$

19) $3\frac{2}{3} \div 1\frac{2}{5} =$

20) $4\frac{1}{4} \div 2\frac{2}{3} =$

21) $3\frac{5}{6} \div 2\frac{4}{5} =$

22) $2\frac{1}{8} \div 1\frac{3}{4} =$

23) $5\frac{1}{2} \div 4\frac{2}{5} =$

24) $6\frac{3}{7} \div 2\frac{1}{7} =$

25) $3\frac{3}{6} \div 1\frac{5}{7} =$

26) $4\frac{4}{9} \div 4\frac{2}{3} =$

Chapter 1: Fractions and Mixed Numbers

Answers – Chapter 1

Simplifying Fractions

1) $\frac{1}{2}$
2) $\frac{1}{3}$
3) $\frac{1}{4}$
4) $\frac{1}{4}$
5) $\frac{1}{3}$
6) $\frac{2}{3}$
7) $\frac{3}{11}$
8) $\frac{4}{9}$
9) $\frac{7}{8}$
10) $\frac{5}{8}$
11) $\frac{1}{2}$
12) $\frac{5}{9}$
13) $\frac{8}{9}$
14) $\frac{9}{11}$
15) $\frac{1}{4}$
16) $\frac{2}{5}$
17) $\frac{1}{2}$
18) $\frac{1}{3}$
19) $\frac{4}{5}$
20) $\frac{8}{9}$
21) $\frac{1}{10}$
22) $\frac{4}{5}$
23) $\frac{6}{7}$
24) $\frac{5}{6}$
25) $\frac{1}{3}$
26) $\frac{1}{3}$

Adding and Subtracting Fractions

1) $\frac{8}{15}$
2) $\frac{31}{40}$
3) $\frac{1}{9}$
4) $\frac{26}{45}$
5) $\frac{5}{9}$
6) $\frac{7}{10}$
7) $\frac{1}{10}$
8) $\frac{22}{63}$
9) $\frac{13}{12}$
10) $\frac{31}{40}$
11) $\frac{7}{20}$
12) $\frac{1}{9}$
13) $\frac{23}{18}$
14) $\frac{11}{12}$
15) $\frac{3}{10}$
16) $\frac{1}{12}$
17) $\frac{22}{15}$
18) $\frac{32}{35}$
19) $\frac{7}{45}$
20) $\frac{17}{45}$
21) $\frac{58}{63}$
22) $\frac{31}{24}$
23) $\frac{11}{35}$
24) $\frac{1}{36}$
25) $\frac{13}{30}$
26) $\frac{15}{28}$

Chapter 1: Fractions and Mixed Numbers

Multiplying and Dividing Fractions

1) $\dfrac{3}{5}$

2) $\dfrac{3}{28}$

3) $\dfrac{4}{5}$

4) $\dfrac{2}{5}$

5) $\dfrac{8}{21}$

6) $\dfrac{15}{28}$

7) $\dfrac{14}{15}$

8) $\dfrac{24}{35}$

9) $\dfrac{3}{14}$

10) $\dfrac{4}{33}$

11) $\dfrac{4}{15}$

12) $\dfrac{3}{8}$

13) $\dfrac{8}{21}$

14) $\dfrac{5}{14}$

15) $\dfrac{77}{54}$

16) $\dfrac{1}{10}$

17) $\dfrac{1}{26}$

18) $\dfrac{1}{21}$

19) $\dfrac{3}{20}$

20) $\dfrac{1}{8}$

21) $\dfrac{5}{14}$

22) $\dfrac{4}{55}$

23) $\dfrac{1}{10}$

24) $\dfrac{1}{10}$

25) $\dfrac{2}{65}$

26) $\dfrac{1}{42}$

Adding Mixed Numbers

1) $3\dfrac{3}{5}$

2) $6\dfrac{1}{3}$

3) $5\dfrac{1}{10}$

4) $5\dfrac{17}{30}$

5) $3\dfrac{7}{30}$

6) $4\dfrac{59}{63}$

7) $5\dfrac{23}{24}$

8) $5\dfrac{5}{63}$

9) $3\dfrac{29}{36}$

10) $6\dfrac{11}{18}$

11) $4\dfrac{1}{2}$

12) $5\dfrac{1}{10}$

13) $5\dfrac{5}{12}$

14) $6\dfrac{13}{22}$

15) $5\dfrac{5}{7}$

16) $5\dfrac{2}{3}$

17) $5\dfrac{16}{25}$

18) $5\dfrac{4}{15}$

19) $8\dfrac{4}{21}$

20) $5\dfrac{7}{8}$

21) $4\dfrac{17}{21}$

22) $5\dfrac{29}{30}$

23) $4\dfrac{29}{56}$

24) $5\dfrac{11}{12}$

25) $3\dfrac{43}{52}$

26) $5\dfrac{27}{35}$

Chapter 1: Fractions and Mixed Numbers

Subtracting Mixed Numbers

1) $3\frac{1}{9}$
2) $3\frac{20}{21}$
3) $2\frac{5}{8}$
4) $4\frac{3}{10}$
5) $2\frac{11}{21}$
6) $1\frac{3}{4}$
7) $1\frac{31}{72}$
8) $2\frac{22}{63}$
9) $1\frac{5}{24}$
10) $2\frac{11}{36}$
11) $4\frac{11}{18}$
12) $1\frac{13}{24}$
13) $1\frac{1}{8}$
14) $2\frac{5}{16}$
15) $2\frac{8}{15}$
16) $1\frac{13}{34}$
17) $3\frac{11}{21}$
18) $1\frac{1}{3}$
19) $2\frac{1}{6}$
20) $2\frac{11}{18}$
21) $4\frac{13}{63}$
22) $1\frac{13}{35}$
23) $4\frac{2}{21}$
24) $2\frac{11}{18}$
25) $2\frac{2}{7}$
26) $4\frac{5}{16}$

Multiplying Mixed Numbers

1) $1\frac{2}{3}$
2) $11\frac{5}{8}$
3) $4\frac{4}{21}$
4) $10\frac{11}{16}$
5) $8\frac{1}{2}$
6) $23\frac{1}{3}$
7) $20\frac{7}{12}$
8) $22\frac{23}{40}$
9) $17\frac{11}{15}$
10) $12\frac{4}{21}$
11) $23\frac{3}{4}$
12) $14\frac{13}{27}$
13) $18\frac{5}{12}$
14) $36\frac{2}{5}$
15) $17\frac{17}{24}$
16) $14\frac{22}{35}$
17) $18\frac{5}{24}$
18) $16\frac{1}{4}$
19) $30\frac{2}{5}$
20) $11\frac{3}{8}$
21) $21\frac{8}{15}$
22) $13\frac{1}{7}$
23) $18\frac{2}{3}$
24) 30
25) $5\frac{31}{40}$
26) $30\frac{2}{3}$

Chapter 1: Fractions and Mixed Numbers

Dividing Mixed Numbers

1) $1\frac{21}{44}$

2) $1\frac{1}{10}$

3) $2\frac{2}{7}$

4) $1\frac{7}{81}$

5) $1\frac{73}{75}$

6) $\frac{42}{55}$

7) $1\frac{77}{95}$

8) $3\frac{3}{80}$

9) $2\frac{53}{140}$

10) $\frac{2}{3}$

11) $2\frac{88}{105}$

12) $\frac{95}{98}$

13) $1\frac{12}{31}$

14) $1\frac{53}{136}$

15) $2\frac{10}{77}$

16) $\frac{64}{95}$

17) $1\frac{47}{68}$

18) $\frac{55}{64}$

19) $2\frac{13}{21}$

20) $1\frac{19}{32}$

21) $1\frac{31}{84}$

22) $1\frac{3}{14}$

23) $1\frac{1}{4}$

24) 3

25) $2\frac{1}{24}$

26) $\frac{20}{21}$

Chapter 2: Decimal

Math Topics that you'll learn in this Chapter:

- ✓ Comparing Decimals
- ✓ Rounding Decimals
- ✓ Adding and Subtracting Decimals
- ✓ Multiplying and Dividing Decimals

Chapter 2: Decimal

Comparing Decimals

✏️ *Compare. Use >, =, and <*

1) 0.44 ☐ 0.044

2) 0.67 ☐ 0.68

3) 0.49 ☐ 0.79

4) 1.35 ☐ 1.45

5) 1.58 ☐ 1.75

6) 2.91 ☐ 2.85

7) 14.56 ☐ 1.456

8) 17.85 ☐ 17.89

9) 21.52 ☐ 21.052

10) 11.12 ☐ 11.03

11) 9.650 ☐ 9.65

12) 8.578 ☐ 8.568

13) 3.15 ☐ 0.315

14) 16.61 ☐ 16.16

15) 18.581 ☐ 8.991

16) 25.05 ☐ 2.505

17) 4.55 ☐ 4.65

18) 0.158 ☐ 1.58

19) 0.881 ☐ 0.871

20) 0.505 ☐ 0.510

21) 0.772 ☐ 0.777

22) 0.5 ☐ 0.500

23) 16.89 ☐ 15.89

24) 12.25 ☐ 12.35

25) 5.82 ☐ 5.69

26) 1.320 ☐ 1.032

27) 0.082 ☐ 0.088

28) 0.99 ☐ 0.099

29) 2.360 ☐ 2.840

30) 0.330 ☐ 0.303

31) 16.44 ☐ 1.664

32) 0.424 ☐ 0.442

Chapter 2: Decimal

Rounding Decimals

✎ Round each number to the underlined place value.

1) 3.960 =

2) 4.372 =

3) 11.136 =

4) 17.5 =

5) 1.981 =

6) 14.215 =

7) 17.548 =

8) 25.508 =

9) 31.089 =

10) 69.345 =

11) 9.457 =

12) 12.901 =

13) 2.658 =

14) 32.565 =

15) 6.058 =

16) 98.108 =

17) 27.705 =

18) 36.75 =

19) 9.08 =

20) 7.185 =

21) 22.547 =

22) 66.098 =

23) 87.75 =

24) 18.541 =

25) 10.258 =

26) 13.456 =

27) 71.084 =

28) 29.23 =

29) 43.45 =

30) 81.07 =

31) 92.366 =

32) 24.76 =

Chapter 2: Decimal

Adding and Subtracting Decimals

✎ Solve.

1) 11.62 + 18.23 =

2) 13.78 + 16.58 =

3) 56.30 − 45.68 =

4) 59.36 − 30.88 =

5) 24.32 + 26.45 =

6) 36.25 + 18.37 =

7) 47.85 − 35.12 =

8) 85.65 − 67.48 =

9) 25.49 + 34.18 =

10) 19.99 + 48.66 =

11) 46.32 − 27.77 =

12) 54.62 − 48.12 =

13) 24.42 + 16.54 =

14) 52.13 + 12.32 =

15) 82.36 − 78.65 =

16) 64.12 − 49.15 =

17) 36.41 + 24.52 =

18) 85.96 − 74.63 =

19) 52.62 − 42.54 =

20) 21.20 + 24.58 =

21) 32.15 + 17.17 =

22) 96.32 − 85.54 =

23) 89.78 − 69.85 =

24) 29.28 + 39.79 =

25) 11.11 + 19.99 =

26) 28.82 + 20.88 =

27) 63.14 − 28.91 =

28) 56.61 − 49.72 =

29) 66.14 + 32.12 =

30) 30.19 + 25.83 =

31) 68.21 − 25.10 =

32) 76.57 − 45.13 =

Chapter 2: Decimal

Multiplying and Dividing Decimals

✎ Solve.

1) $12.3 \times 0.2 =$

2) $12.6 \times 0.9 =$

3) $54.4 \div 2 =$

4) $64.8 \div 8 =$

5) $23.1 \times 0.3 =$

6) $1.2 \times 0.7 =$

7) $5.5 \div 0.5 =$

8) $64.8 \div 8 =$

9) $1.4 \times 0.5 =$

10) $4.5 \times 0.3 =$

11) $88.8 \div 4 =$

12) $10.5 \div 5 =$

13) $2.2 \times 0.3 =$

14) $0.2 \times 0.52 =$

15) $95.7 \div 100 =$

16) $36.6 \div 6 =$

17) $3.2 \times 2 =$

18) $4.1 \times 0.5 =$

19) $68.4 \div 2 =$

20) $27.9 \div 9 =$

21) $3.5 \times 4 =$

22) $4.8 \times 0.5 =$

23) $6.4 \div 4 =$

24) $72.8 \div 0.8 =$

25) $1.8 \times 3 =$

26) $6.5 \times 0.2 =$

27) $93.6 \div 3 =$

28) $45.15 \div 0.5 =$

29) $12.6 \times 0.5 =$

30) $13.2 \times 6 =$

31) $6.4 \div 0.8 =$

32) $98.6 \div 0.2 =$

Chapter 2: Decimal

Answers – Chapter 2

Comparing Decimals

1) $0.44 > 0.044$

2) $0.67 < 0.68$

3) $0.49 < 0.79$

4) $1.35 < 1.45$

5) $1.58 < 1.75$

6) $2.91 > 2.85$

7) $14.56 > 1.456$

8) $17.85 < 17.89$

9) $21.52 > 21.052$

10) $11.12 > 11.03$

11) $9.650 = 9.65$

12) $8.578 > 8.568$

13) $3.15 > 0.315$

14) $16.61 > 16.16$

15) $18.581 > 8.991$

16) $25.05 > 2.505$

17) $4.55 < 4.65$

18) $0.158 < 1.58$

19) $0.881 > 0.871$

20) $0.505 < 0.510$

21) $0.772 < 0.777$

22) $0.5 = 0.500$

23) $16.89 > 15.89$

24) $12.25 < 12.35$

25) $5.82 > 5.69$

26) $1.320 > 1.032$

27) $0.082 < 0.088$

28) $0.99 > 0.099$

29) $2.360 < 2.840$

30) $0.330 > 0.303$

31) $16.44 > 1.664$

32) $0.424 < 0.442$

Chapter 2: Decimal

Rounding Decimals

1) 3.960 = 4

2) 4.372 = 4.37

3) 11.136 = 11.14

4) 17.5 = 18

5) 1.981 = 1.98

6) 14.215 = 14.2

7) 17.548 = 17.55

8) 25.508 = 25.51

9) 31.089 = 31

10) 69.345 = 69.3

11) 9.457 = 9.46

12) 12.901 = 13

13) 2.658 = 2.66

14) 32.565 = 32.6

15) 6.058 = 6.06

16) 98.108 = 98.11

17) 27.705 = 27.7

18) 36.75 = 37

19) 9.08 = 9.1

20) 7.185 = 7.2

21) 22.547 = 22.55

22) 66.098 = 66.1

23) 87.75 = 88

24) 18.541 = 18.5

25) 10.258 = 10.26

26) 13.456 = 13.5

27) 71.084 = 71.08

28) 29.23 = 29

29) 43.45 = 43.5

30) 81.07 = 81

31) 92.366 = 92

32) 24.76 = 24.8

Chapter 2: Decimal

Adding and Subtracting Decimals

1) 29.85
2) 30.36
3) 10.62
4) 28.48
5) 50.77
6) 54.62
7) 12.73
8) 18.17
9) 59.67
10) 68.65
11) 18.55
12) 6.5
13) 40.96
14) 64.45
15) 3.71
16) 14.97
17) 60.93
18) 11.33
19) 10.08
20) 45.78
21) 49.32
22) 10.78
23) 19.93
24) 69.07
25) 31.1
26) 49.7
27) 34.23
28) 6.89
29) 98.26
30) 56.02
31) 43.11
32) 31.44

Multiplying and Dividing Decimals

1) 2.46
2) 11.34
3) 27.2
4) 8.1
5) 6.93
6) 0.84
7) 11
8) 8.1
9) 0.7
10) 1.35
11) 22.2
12) 2.1
13) 0.66
14) 0.104
15) 0.957
16) 6.1
17) 6.4
18) 2.05
19) 34.2
20) 3.1
21) 14
22) 2.4
23) 1.6
24) 91
25) 5.4
26) 1.3
27) 31.2
28) 90.3
29) 6.3
30) 79.2
31) 8
32) 493

Chapter 3: Integers and Order of Operations

Math Topics that you'll learn in this Chapter:

- ✓ Adding and Subtracting Integers
- ✓ Multiplying and Dividing Integers
- ✓ Order of Operations
- ✓ Integers and Absolute Value

Chapter 3: Integers and Order of Operations

Adding and Subtracting Integers

✎ Solve.

1) $-(9) + 15 =$

2) $15 - (-11 - 9) =$

3) $(-10) + (-6) =$

4) $(-10) + (-6) + 7 =$

5) $-(23) + 19 =$

6) $(-7 + 5) - 9 =$

7) $28 + (-32) =$

8) $(-11) + (-9) + 5 =$

9) $25 - (8 - 7) =$

10) $-(29) + 17 =$

11) $(-38) + (-3) + 29 =$

12) $15 - (-7 + 9) =$

13) $24 - (8 - 2) =$

14) $(-7 + 4) - 9 =$

15) $(-17) + (-3) + 9 =$

16) $(-26) + (-7) + 8 =$

17) $(-9) + (-11) =$

18) $8 - (-23 - 13) =$

19) $(-16) + (-2) =$

20) $25 - (7 - 4) =$

21) $23 + (-12) =$

22) $(-18) + (-6) =$

23) $17 - (-21 - 7) =$

24) $-(28) - (-16) + 5 =$

25) $(-9 + 4) - 8 =$

26) $(-28) + (-6) + 17 =$

27) $-(21) - (-15) + 9 =$

28) $(-31) + (-6) =$

29) $(-18) + (-10) + 13 =$

30) $(-30) + (-11) + 12 =$

31) $-(28) - (-10) + 6 =$

32) $6 - (-16 - 11) =$

Chapter 3: Integers and Order of Operations

Multiplying and Dividing Integers

✏️ **Solve.**

1) $(-6) \times (-7) =$

2) $8 \times (-5) =$

3) $48 \div (-8) =$

4) $(-72) \div 9 =$

5) $(4) \times (-6) =$

6) $(-9) \times (-11) =$

7) $(10) \div (-5) =$

8) $144 \div (-12) =$

9) $(10) \times (-2) =$

10) $(-8) \times (-2) \times 5 =$

11) $(8) \div (-2) =$

12) $45 \div (-15) =$

13) $(5) \times (-7) =$

14) $(-6) \times (-5) \times 4 =$

15) $(12) \div (-6) =$

16) $(14) \div (-7) =$

17) $196 \div (-14) =$

18) $(27 - 13) \times (-2) =$

19) $125 \div (-5) =$

20) $66 \div (-6) =$

21) $(-6) \times (-5) \times 3 =$

22) $(15 - 6) \times (-3) =$

23) $(32 - 24) \div (-4) =$

24) $72 \div (-6) =$

25) $(-14 + 8) \times (-7) =$

26) $(-3) \times (-9) \times 3 =$

27) $84 \div (-12) =$

28) $(-12) \times (-10) =$

29) $22 \times (-3) =$

30) $(-2) \times (-6) \times 5 =$

31) $(24) \div (-3) =$

32) $(-15) \div (3) =$

Chapter 3: Integers and Order of Operations

Order of Operation

✏️ *Calculate.*

1) $16 + (30 \div 5) =$

2) $(3 \times 9) \div (-3) =$

3) $57 - (3 \times 8) =$

4) $(-12) \times (7 - 3) =$

5) $(18 - 7) \times (6) =$

6) $(6 \times 10) \div (12 + 3) =$

7) $(13 \times 2) - (24 \div 6) =$

8) $(-5) + (4 \times 3) + 8 =$

9) $(4 \times 2^3) + (16 - 9) =$

10) $(3^2 \times 7) \div (-2 + 1) =$

11) $[-2(48 \div 2^3)] - 6 =$

12) $(-4) + (7 \times 8) + 18 =$

13) $(3 \times 7) + (16 - 7) =$

14) $[3^3 \times (48 \div 2^3)] \div (-2) =$

15) $(14 \times 3) - (3^4 \div 9) =$

16) $(96 \div 12) \times (-3) =$

17) $(48 \div 2^2) \times (-2) =$

18) $(56 \div 7) \times (-5) =$

19) $(-2^2) + (7 \times 9) - 21 =$

20) $(2^4 - 9) \times (-6) =$

21) $[4^3 \times (50 \div 5^2)] \div (-16) =$

22) $(3^2 \times 4^2) \div (-4 + 2) =$

23) $6^2 - (-6 \times 4) + 3 =$

24) $4^2 - (5^2 \times 3) =$

25) $(-4) + (12^2 \div 3^2) - 7^2 =$

26) $(3^2 \times 5) + (-5^2 - 9) =$

27) $2[(3^2 \times 5) \times (-6)] =$

28) $(11^2 - 2^2) - (-7^2) =$

29) $(2^2 \times 5) - (64 \div 8) =$

30) $2[(3^2 \times 4) + (35 \div 5)] =$

31) $(4^2 \times 3) \div (-6) =$

32) $3^2[(4^3 \div 16) - (3^3 \div 27)] =$

Chapter 3: Integers and Order of Operations

Integers and Absolute Value

✍ **Calculate.**

1) $4 - |6 - 10| =$

2) $|14| - \frac{|-18|}{3} =$

3) $\frac{|8 \times -8|}{4} \times \frac{|-20|}{5} =$

4) $|12 \times 3| + \frac{|-81|}{9} =$

5) $4 - |11 - 18| - |3| =$

6) $|18| - \frac{|-12|}{4} =$

7) $\frac{|5 \times -8|}{10} \times \frac{|-22|}{11} =$

8) $|9 \times 3| + \frac{|-36|}{4} =$

9) $|-42 + 7| \times \frac{|-2 \times 5|}{10} =$

10) $6 - |17 - 11| - |5| =$

11) $|13| - \frac{|-54|}{6} =$

12) $\frac{|9 \times -4|}{12} \times \frac{|-45|}{9} =$

13) $|-75 + 50| \times \frac{|-4 \times 5|}{5} =$

14) $\frac{|-26|}{13} \times \frac{|-32|}{8} =$

15) $14 - |8 - 18| - |-12| =$

16) $|29| - \frac{|-20|}{5} =$

17) $\frac{|3 \times 8|}{2} \times \frac{|-33|}{3} =$

18) $|-45 + 15| \times \frac{|-12 \times 5|}{6} =$

19) $\frac{|-50|}{5} \times \frac{|-77|}{11} =$

20) $12 - |2 - 7| - |15| =$

21) $|18| - \frac{|-45|}{15} =$

22) $\frac{|7 \times 8|}{4} \times \frac{|-48|}{12} =$

23) $\frac{|30 \times 2|}{3} \times |-12| =$

24) $\frac{|-36|}{9} \times \frac{|-80|}{8} =$

25) $|-30 + 9| \times \frac{|-8 \times 5|}{8} =$

26) $|16| - \frac{|-18|}{3} =$

27) $12 - |10 - 24| + |5| =$

28) $|-38 + 8| \times \frac{|-5 \times 6|}{10} =$

Chapter 3: Integers and Order of Operations

Answers – Chapter 3

Adding and Subtracting Integers

1) 6
2) 35
3) −16
4) −9
5) −4
6) −11
7) −4
8) −15
9) 24
10) −12
11) −12
12) 13
13) 18
14) −12
15) −11
16) −25
17) −20
18) 44
19) −18
20) 22
21) 11
22) −24
23) 45
24) −7
25) −13
26) −17
27) 3
28) −37
29) −15
30) −29
31) −12
32) 33

Multiplying and Dividing Integers

1) 42
2) −40
3) −6
4) −8
5) −24
6) 99
7) −2
8) −12
9) −20
10) 80
11) −4
12) −3
13) −35
14) 120
15) −2
16) −2
17) −14
18) −28
19) −25
20) −11
21) 90
22) −27
23) −2
24) −12
25) 42
26) 81
27) −7
28) 120
29) −66
30) 60
31) −8
32) −5

Chapter 3: Integers and Order of Operations

Order of Operation

1) 22
2) −9
3) 33
4) −48
5) 66
6) 4
7) 22
8) 15
9) 39
10) −63
11) −18
12) 70
13) 30
14) −81
15) 33
16) −24
17) −24
18) −40
19) 38
20) −42
21) −8
22) −72
23) 63
24) −59
25) −37
26) 11
27) −540
28) 166
29) 12
30) 86
31) −8
32) 27

Integers and Absolute Value

1) 0
2) 8
3) 64
4) 45
5) −6
6) 15
7) 8
8) 36
9) 35
10) −5
11) 4
12) 15
13) 100
14) 8
15) −8
16) 25
17) 132
18) 300
19) 70
20) −8
21) 15
22) 56
23) 240
24) 40
25) 105
26) 10
27) 3
28) 90

Chapter 4: Ratios and Proportions

Math Topics that you'll learn in this Chapter:

- ✓ Simplifying Ratios
- ✓ Proportional Ratios
- ✓ Similarity and Ratios
- ✓ Simple Interest

Chapter 4: Ratios and Proportions

Simplifying Ratios

✎ *Simplify each ratio.*

1) $3:21 = \underline{} : \underline{}$

2) $4:16 = \underline{} : \underline{}$

3) $\frac{2}{28} = -$

4) $\frac{18}{45} = -$

5) $10:30 = \underline{} : \underline{}$

6) $5:30 = \underline{} : \underline{}$

7) $\frac{34}{38} = -$

8) $\frac{45}{63} = -$

9) $10:45 = \underline{} : \underline{}$

10) $20:30 = \underline{} : \underline{}$

11) $\frac{40}{64} = -$

12) $\frac{10}{110} = -$

13) $8:12 = \underline{} : \underline{}$

14) $16:20 = \underline{} : \underline{}$

15) $\frac{24}{48} = -$

16) $\frac{21}{77} = -$

17) $8:24 = \underline{} : \underline{}$

18) $9 \text{ to } 36 = \underline{} : \underline{}$

19) $\frac{64}{72} = -$

20) $\frac{45}{60} = -$

21) $12:15 = \underline{} : \underline{}$

22) $18:54 = \underline{} : \underline{}$

23) $\frac{36}{54} = -$

24) $\frac{48}{104} = -$

25) $12:48 = \underline{} : \underline{}$

26) $18:72 = \underline{} : \underline{}$

27) $\frac{15}{75} = -$

28) $\frac{46}{52} = -$

Chapter 4: Ratios and Proportions

Proportional Ratios

✎ *Solve each proportion for x.*

1) $\frac{4}{7} = \frac{8}{x}$, $x = $ _____

2) $\frac{9}{12} = \frac{x}{8}$, $x = $ _____

3) $\frac{3}{5} = \frac{12}{x}$, $x = $ _____

4) $\frac{3}{10} = \frac{x}{50}$, $x = $ _____

5) $\frac{3}{11} = \frac{15}{x}$, $x = $ _____

6) $\frac{6}{15} = \frac{x}{45}$, $x = $ _____

7) $\frac{6}{19} = \frac{12}{x}$, $x = $ _____

8) $\frac{7}{16} = \frac{x}{32}$, $x = $ _____

9) $\frac{18}{21} = \frac{54}{x}$, $x = $ _____

10) $\frac{13}{15} = \frac{39}{x}$, $x = $ _____

11) $\frac{9}{13} = \frac{72}{x}$, $x = $ _____

12) $\frac{8}{30} = \frac{x}{180}$, $x = $ _____

13) $\frac{3}{19} = \frac{9}{x}$, $x = $ _____

14) $\frac{1}{3} = \frac{x}{90}$, $x = $ _____

15) $\frac{25}{45} = \frac{x}{9}$, $x = $ _____

16) $\frac{1}{6} = \frac{9}{x}$, $x = $ _____

17) $\frac{7}{9} = \frac{63}{x}$, $x = $ _____

18) $\frac{54}{72} = \frac{x}{8}$, $x = $ _____

19) $\frac{32}{40} = \frac{4}{x}$, $x = $ _____

20) $\frac{21}{42} = \frac{x}{6}$, $x = $ _____

21) $\frac{56}{72} = \frac{7}{x}$, $x = $ _____

22) $\frac{1}{14} = \frac{x}{42}$, $x = $ _____

23) $\frac{5}{7} = \frac{75}{x}$, $x = $ _____

24) $\frac{30}{48} = \frac{x}{8}$, $x = $ _____

25) $\frac{36}{88} = \frac{9}{x}$, $x = $ _____

26) $\frac{62}{68} = \frac{x}{34}$, $x = $ _____

27) $\frac{42}{60} = \frac{x}{10}$, $x = $ _____

28) $\frac{8}{9} = \frac{x}{108}$, $x = $ _____

29) $\frac{40}{6} = \frac{x}{3}$, $x = $ _____

30) $\frac{88}{121} = \frac{x}{11}$, $x = $ _____

31) $\frac{10}{24} = \frac{x}{48}$, $x = $ _____

32) $\frac{32}{80} = \frac{x}{10}$, $x = $ _____

Chapter 4: Ratios and Proportions

Create Proportion

✏️ *State if each pair of ratios form a proportion.*

1) $\dfrac{3}{8}$ and $\dfrac{24}{50}$

2) $\dfrac{3}{11}$ and $\dfrac{6}{22}$

3) $\dfrac{4}{5}$ and $\dfrac{16}{20}$

4) $\dfrac{5}{11}$ and $\dfrac{12}{33}$

5) $\dfrac{5}{10}$ and $\dfrac{15}{30}$

6) $\dfrac{4}{13}$ and $\dfrac{8}{24}$

7) $\dfrac{6}{9}$ and $\dfrac{24}{36}$

8) $\dfrac{7}{12}$ and $\dfrac{14}{20}$

9) $\dfrac{3}{8}$ and $\dfrac{27}{72}$

10) $\dfrac{12}{20}$ and $\dfrac{36}{60}$

11) $\dfrac{11}{12}$ and $\dfrac{55}{60}$

12) $\dfrac{12}{15}$ and $\dfrac{24}{25}$

13) $\dfrac{15}{19}$ and $\dfrac{20}{38}$

14) $\dfrac{10}{14}$ and $\dfrac{40}{56}$

15) $\dfrac{11}{13}$ and $\dfrac{44}{39}$

16) $\dfrac{15}{16}$ and $\dfrac{30}{32}$

17) $\dfrac{17}{19}$ and $\dfrac{34}{48}$

18) $\dfrac{5}{18}$ and $\dfrac{15}{54}$

19) $\dfrac{3}{14}$ and $\dfrac{18}{42}$

20) $\dfrac{7}{11}$ and $\dfrac{14}{32}$

21) $\dfrac{8}{11}$ and $\dfrac{32}{44}$

22) $\dfrac{8}{14}$ and $\dfrac{24}{54}$

✏️ *Solve.*

23) The ratio of boys to girls in a class is 3: 4. If there are 27 boys in the class, how many girls are in that class? _____

24) The ratio of red marbles to blue marbles in a bag is 5: 6. If there are 66 marbles in the bag, how many of the marbles are red? _____

25) You can buy 6 cans of green beans at a supermarket for $3.60. How much does it cost to buy 48 cans of green beans? _____

Chapter 4: Ratios and Proportions

Similarity and Ratios

✎ *Each pair of figures is similar. Find the missing side.*

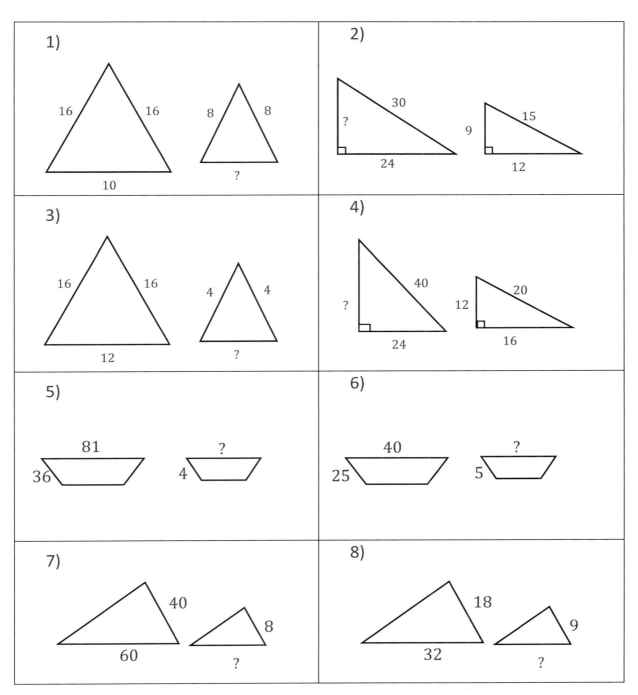

Chapter 4: Ratios and Proportions

Simple Interest

✏️ *Determine the simple interest for these loans.*

1) $400 at 6% for 4 years. $___
2) $580 at 3.5% for 5 years. $___
3) $320 at 4% for 6 years. $___
4) $510 at 8% for 3 years. $___
5) $690 at 5% for 6 months. $___
6) $620 at 7% for 3 years. $___
7) $650 at 4.5% for 10 years. $___
8) $850 at 4% for 2 years. $___
9) $640 at 7% for 3 years. $___
10) $300 at 9% for 9 months. $___
11) $760 at 8% for 2 years. $___
12) $910 at 5% for 5 years. $___
13) $540 at 3% for 6 years. $___
14) $780 at 2.5% for 4 years. $___
15) $1,600 at 7% for 3 months. $___
16) $310 at 4% for 4 years. $___
17) $950 at 6% for 5 years. $___
18) $280 at 8% for 7 years. $___
19) $310 at 6% for 3 years. $___
20) $990 at 5% for 4 months. $___

21) $380 at 6% for 5 years. $___
22) $580 at 6% for 4 years. $___
23) $1,200 at 4% for 5 years. $___
24) $3,100 at 5% for 6 years. $___
25) $5,200 at 8% for 2 years. $___
26) $1,400 at 4% for 3 years. $___
27) $300 at 3% for 8 months. $___
28) $150 at 3.5% for 4 years. $___
29) $170 at 6% for 2 years. $___
30) $940 at 8% for 5 years. $___
31) $960 at 1.5% for 8 years. $___
32) $240 at 5% for 4 months. $___
33) $280 at 2% for 5 years. $___
34) $880 at 3% for 2 years. $___
35) $2,200 at 4.5% for 2 years. $___
36) $2,400 at 7% for 3 years. $___
37) $1,800 at 5% for 6 months. $___
38) $190 at 4% for 2 years. $___
39) $480 at 6% for 5 years. $___
40) $700 at 5% for 6 years. $___

Chapter 4: Ratios and Proportions

Answers – Chapter 4

Simplifying Ratios

1) $1:7$
2) $1:4$
3) $\frac{1}{14}$
4) $\frac{2}{5}$
5) $1:3$
6) $1:6$
7) $\frac{17}{19}$
8) $\frac{5}{7}$
9) $2:9$
10) $2:3$
11) $\frac{5}{8}$
12) $\frac{1}{11}$
13) $2:3$
14) $4:5$
15) $\frac{1}{2}$
16) $\frac{3}{11}$
17) $1:3$
18) 1 to 4
19) $\frac{8}{9}$
20) $\frac{3}{4}$
21) $4:5$
22) $1:3$
23) $\frac{2}{3}$
24) $\frac{6}{13}$
25) $1:4$
26) $1:4$
27) $\frac{1}{5}$
28) $\frac{23}{26}$

Proportional Ratios

1) $x = 14$
2) $x = 6$
3) $x = 20$
4) $x = 15$
5) $x = 55$
6) $x = 18$
7) $x = 38$
8) $x = 14$
9) $x = 63$
10) $x = 45$
11) $x = 104$
12) $x = 48$
13) $x = 57$
14) $x = 30$
15) $x = 5$
16) $x = 54$
17) $x = 81$
18) $x = 6$
19) $x = 5$
20) $x = 3$
21) $x = 9$
22) $x = 3$
23) $x = 105$
24) $x = 5$
25) $x = 22$
26) $x = 31$
27) $x = 7$
28) $x = 96$
29) $x = 20$
30) $x = 8$
31) $x = 20$
32) $x = 4$

Chapter 4: Ratios and Proportions

Create Proportion

1) No
2) Yes
3) Yes
4) No
5) Yes
6) No
7) Yes
8) No
9) Yes
10) Yes
11) Yes
12) No
13) No
14) Yes
15) No
16) Yes
17) No
18) Yes
19) No
20) No
21) Yes
22) No
23) 36 girls
24) 30 red marbles
25) $28.80

Similarity and Ratios

1) 5
2) 18
3) 3
4) 32
5) 9
6) 8
7) 12
8) 16

Chapter 4: Ratios and Proportions

Simple Interest

1) $96
2) $101.50
3) $76.80
4) $122.40
5) $17.25
6) $130.20
7) $292.50
8) $68
9) $134.40
10) $20.25
11) $121.60
12) $227.50
13) $97.20
14) $78
15) $28
16) $49.60
17) $285
18) $156.80
19) $55.80
20) $16.5
21) $114
22) $139.20
23) $240
24) $930
25) $832
26) $168
27) $6
28) $21
29) $20.40
30) $376
31) $115.20
32) $4
33) $28
34) $52.80
35) $198
36) $504
37) $45
38) $15.20
39) $144
40) $210

Chapter 5: Percentage

Math Topics that you'll learn in this Chapter:

- ✓ Percent Problems
- ✓ Percent of Increase and Decrease
- ✓ Discount, Tax and Tip

Chapter 5: Percentage

Percent Problems

Solve each problem.

1) What is 4 percent of 280? ____
2) What is 25 percent of 500? ____
3) What is 10 percent of 460? ____
4) What is 34 percent of 260? ____
5) What is 60 percent of 850? ____
6) 63 is what percent of 300? ____%
7) 80 is what percent of 400? ____%
8) 70 is what percent of 700? ____%
9) 84 is what percent of 600? ____%
10) 90 is what percent of 300? ____%
11) 24 is what percent of 150? ____%
12) 12 is what percent of 80? ____%
13) 4 is what percent of 50? ____%
14) 110 is what percent of 500? ____%
15) 16 is what percent of 400? ____%

16) 39 is what percent of 300? ____%
17) 56 is what percent of 200? ____%
18) 30 is what percent of 500? ____%
19) 84 is what percent of 700? ____%
20) 40 is what percent of 500? ____%
21) 26 is what percent of 100? ____%
22) 45 is what percent of 900? ____%
23) 60 is what percent of 400? ____%
24) 18 is what percent of 900? ____%
25) 75 is what percent of 250? ____%
26) 27 is what percent of 900? ____%
27) 49 is what percent of 700? ____%
28) 81 is what percent of 900? ____%
29) 90 is what percent of 500? ____%
30) 82 is what percent of 410? ____%

31) 14 is 35 percent of what number? ____
32) 90 is 6 percent of what number? ____
33) 80 is 40 percent of what number? ____
34) 80 is 20 percent of what number? ____
35) 30 is 6 percent of what number? ____
36) 64 is 8 percent of what number? ____

Chapter 5: Percentage

Percent of Increase and Decrease

✍ *Solve each percent of change word problem.*

1) Bob got a raise, and his hourly wage increased from $30 to $42. What is the percent increase? _____ %

2) The price of gasoline rose from $4.40 to $4.62 in one month. By what percent did the gas price rise? _____ %

3) In a class, the number of students has been increased from 25 to 32. What is the percent increase? _____ %

4) The price of a pair of shoes increases from $24 to $30. What is the percent increase? ___ %

5) In a class, the number of students has been decreased from 24 to 18. What is the percentage decrease? _____ %

6) Nick got a raise, and his hourly wage increased from $50 to $55. What is the percent increase? _____ %

7) A coat was originally priced at $60. It went on sale for $54. What was the percent that the coat was discounted? _____ %

8) The price of a pair of shoes increases from $12 to $18. What is the percent increase? ___ %

9) A house was purchased in 2002 for $150,000. It is now valued at $132,000. What is the rate (percent) of depreciation for the house? ____ %

10) The price of gasoline rose from $4.00 to $4.20 in one month. By what percent did the gas price rise? _____ %

Chapter 5: Percentage

Discount, Tax and Tip

🖎 *Find the missing values.*

1) Original price of a computer: $540, Tax: 6%, Selling price: $_____

2) Original price of a sofa: $400, Tax: 14%, Selling price: $_____

3) Original price of a table: $560, Tax: 15%, Selling price: $_____

4) Original price of a cell phone: $740, Tax: 24%, Selling price: $_____

5) Original price of a printer: $400, Tax: 22%, Selling price: $_____

6) Original price of a computer: $600, Tax: 15%, Selling price: $_____

7) Restaurant bill: $24.00, Tip: 25%, Final amount: $_____

8) Original price of a cell phone: $300 Tax: 8%, Selling price: $_____

9) Original price of a carpet: $800, Tax: 25%, Selling price: $_____

10) Original price of a camera: $200 Discount: 35%, Selling price: $_____

11) Original price of a dress: $560 Discount: 10%, Selling price: $_____

12) Original price of a monitor: $420 Discount: 6%, Selling price: $_____

13) Original price of a laptop: $880 Discount: 16%, Selling price: $_____

14) Restaurant bill: $64.00, Tip: 20%, Final amount: $_____

Chapter 5: Percentage

Answers – Chapter 5

Percent Problems

1) 11.2
2) 125
3) 46
4) 88.4
5) 510
6) 21%
7) 20%
8) 10%
9) 14%
10) 30%
11) 16%
12) 15%
13) 8%
14) 22%
15) 4%
16) 13%
17) 28%
18) 6%
19) 12%
20) 8%
21) 26%
22) 5%
23) 15%
24) 2%
25) 30%
26) 3%
27) 7%
28) 9%
29) 18%
30) 20%
31) 40
32) 1,500
33) 200
34) 400
35) 500
36) 800

Percent of Increase and Decrease

1) 40%
2) 5%
3) 28%
4) 25%
5) 25%
6) 10%
7) 10%
8) 50%
9) 12%
10) 5%

Chapter 5: Percentage

Discount, Tax and Tip

1) $572.40

2) $456

3) $644

4) $917.60

5) $488

6) $690

7) $30.00

8) $324

9) $1,000

10) $130

11) $504

12) $394.8

13) $739.2

14) $76.80

Chapter 6: Expressions and Variables

Math Topics that you'll learn in this Chapter:

- ✓ Simplifying Variable Expressions
- ✓ Simplifying Polynomial Expressions
- ✓ Evaluating One Variable
- ✓ Evaluating Two Variables
- ✓ The Distributive Property

Chapter 6: Expressions and Variables

Simplifying Variable Expressions

✏️ *Simplify and write the answer.*

1) $6x + 2 + 3x =$

2) $7x + 4 - 6x =$

3) $-1 - x^2 - 9x^2 =$

4) $(-5)(6x - 2) =$

5) $3 + 10x^2 + 2x =$

6) $8x^2 + 6x + 7x^2 =$

7) $2x^2 - 5x - 7x =$

8) $x - 3 + 5 - 3x =$

9) $2 - 3x + 12 - 2x =$

10) $5x^2 - 12x^2 + 8x =$

11) $2x^2 + 6x + 3x^2 =$

12) $2x^2 - 2x - x =$

13) $2x^2 - (-8x + 6) =$

14) $4x + 6(2 - 5x) =$

15) $10x + 8(10x - 6) =$

16) $9(-2x - 6) - 5 =$

17) $32x - 4 + 23 + 2x =$

18) $8x - 12x - x^2 + 13 =$

19) $(-6)(8x - 4) + 10x =$

20) $14x - 5(5 - 8x) =$

21) $23x + 4(9x + 3) + 12 =$

22) $3(-7x + 5) + 20x =$

23) $12x - 3x(x + 9) =$

24) $7x + 5x(3 - 3x) =$

25) $5x(-8x + 12) + 14x =$

26) $40x + 12 + 2x^2 =$

27) $5x(x - 3) - 10 =$

28) $8x - 7 + 8x + 2x^2 =$

29) $6x - 2x^2 - 6x^2 - 5 =$

30) $3 + x^2 - 4x^2 - 10x =$

31) $10x + 6x^2 + 5x + 18 =$

32) $20 + 12x^2 + 7x - 6x^2 =$

Chapter 6: Expressions and Variables

Simplifying Polynomial Expressions

✎ **Simplify and write the answer.**

1) $(3x^3 + 4x^2) - (10x + 3x^2) =$ _____

2) $(-4x^5 + 4x^3) - (6x^3 + 5x^2) =$ _____

3) $(10x^4 + 6x^2) - (x^2 - 8x^4) =$ _____

4) $6x - 2x^2 - 3(2x^2 + 5x^3) =$ _____

5) $(2x^3 - 3) + 3(2x^2 - 3x^3) =$ _____

6) $4(4x^3 - 2x) - (3x^3 - 2x^4) =$ _____

7) $2(4x - 3x^3) - 3(3x^3 + 4x^2) =$ _____

8) $(2x^2 - 2x) - (2x^3 + 5x^2) =$ _____

9) $2x^3 - (4x^4 + 2x) + x^2 =$ _____

10) $x^4 - 9(x^2 + x) - 5x =$ _____

11) $(-2x^2 - x^4) + (4x^4 - x^2) =$ _____

12) $4x^2 - 5x^3 + 15x^4 - 12x^3 =$ _____

13) $3x^2 - 2x^4 + 12x^4 - 10x^3 =$ _____

14) $4x^2 + 6x^3 - 8x^2 + 14x =$ _____

15) $3x^4 - 6x^5 + 7x^4 - 9x^2 =$ _____

16) $5x^3 + 15x - 4x^2 - 3x^3 =$ _____

Chapter 6: Expressions and Variables

Evaluating One Variable

✏️ *Evaluate each expression using the value given.*

1) $x = 2 \Rightarrow 5x - 10 =$

2) $x = 3 \Rightarrow 6x - 12 =$

3) $x = 4 \Rightarrow 6x + 8 =$

4) $x = 6 \Rightarrow 2x + 4 =$

5) $x = 4 \Rightarrow 4x - 8 =$

6) $x = 2 \Rightarrow 5x - 2x + 10 =$

7) $x = 3 \Rightarrow 2x - x - 6 =$

8) $x = 4 \Rightarrow 6x - 3x + 4 =$

9) $x = -2 \Rightarrow 4x - 6x - 5 =$

10) $x = -1 \Rightarrow 3x - 5x + 11 =$

11) $x = 1 \Rightarrow x - 7x + 12 =$

12) $x = 2 \Rightarrow 2(-3x + 4) =$

13) $x = 3 \Rightarrow 4(-5x - 2) =$

14) $x = 2 \Rightarrow 5(-2x - 4) =$

15) $x = -2 \Rightarrow 3(-4x - 5) =$

16) $x = 3 \Rightarrow 8x + 5 =$

17) $x = -3 \Rightarrow 12x + 9 =$

18) $x = -1 \Rightarrow 9x - 8 =$

19) $x = 2 \Rightarrow 16x - 10 =$

20) $x = 1 \Rightarrow 4x + 3 =$

21) $x = 5 \Rightarrow 7x - 2 =$

22) $x = 7 \Rightarrow 28 - x =$

23) $x = 8 \Rightarrow 4x - 12 =$

24) $x = 10 \Rightarrow 44 - 3x =$

25) $x = 4 \Rightarrow 10x - 6 =$

26) $x = 7 \Rightarrow 6x - x + 9 =$

Chapter 6: Expressions and Variables

Evaluating Two Variables

✎ **Evaluate each expression using the values given.**

1) $x + 4y, x = 3, y = 2$ _____

2) $6x + 3y, x = -2, y = -3$ _____

3) $x + 5y, x = 2, y = -1$ _____

4) $3a - (10 - b), a = 3, b = 4$ _____

5) $4a - (6 - 3b), a = 1, b = 4$ _____

6) $a - (8 - 2b), a = 2, b = 5$ _____

7) $3z + 21 + 5k, z = 4, k = 1$ _____

8) $-7a + 4b, a = 6, b = 3$ _____

9) $-4a + 3b, a = 2, b = 4$ _____

10) $-6a + 6b, a = 4, b = 3$ _____

11) $-8a + 2b, a = 4, b = 6$ _____

12) $4x + 6y, x = 6, y = 3$ _____

13) $2x + 9y, x = 8, y = 1$ _____

14) $x - 7y, x = 9, y = 4$ _____

15) $5x - 4y, x = 6, y = 3$ _____

16) $2z + 14 + 8k, z = 4, k = 1$ _____

17) $6x + 3y, x = 3, y = 8$ _____

18) $5a - 6b, a = -3, b = -1$ _____

19) $6a + 2b, a = -6, b = 4$ _____

20) $-3a - b, a = 5, b = -6$ _____

21) $-6a + 2b, a = 6, b = -3$ _____

22) $-6a + 8b, a = 6, b = -1$ _____

Chapter 6: Expressions and Variables

The Distributive Property

✏️ *Use the distributive property to simply each expression.*

1) $(-2)(10x + 3) =$

2) $(-3x + 5)(-5) =$

3) $11(-3x + 3) =$

4) $6(5 - 4x) =$

5) $(6 - 5x)(-4) =$

6) $9(8 - 2x) =$

7) $(-4x + 6)5 =$

8) $(-2x + 7)(-8) =$

9) $8(-4x + 7) =$

10) $(-9x + 5)(-3) =$

11) $8(-x + 9) =$

12) $7(2 - 6x) =$

13) $(-12x + 4)(-3) =$

14) $(-6)(-10x + 6) =$

15) $(-5)(5 - 11x) =$

16) $9(4 - 8x) =$

17) $(-6x + 2)7 =$

18) $(-9)(1 - 12x) =$

19) $(-3)(4 - 6x) =$

20) $(2 - 8x)(-2) =$

21) $20(2 - x) =$

22) $12(-4x + 3) =$

23) $12(3 - 4x) =$

24) $(-6x + 6)3 =$

25) $(-10x + 6)(-3) =$

26) $13(4 - 7x) =$

Chapter 6: Expressions and Variables

Answers – Chapter 6

Simplifying Variable Expressions

1) $9x + 2$

2) $x + 4$

3) $-10x^2 - 1$

4) $-30x + 10$

5) $10x^2 + 2x + 3$

6) $15x^2 + 6x$

7) $2x^2 - 12x$

8) $-2x + 2$

9) $-5x + 14$

10) $-7x^2 + 8x$

11) $5x^2 + 6x$

12) $2x^2 - 3x$

13) $2x^2 + 8x - 6$

14) $-26x + 12$

15) $90x - 48$

16) $-18x - 59$

17) $34x + 19$

18) $-x^2 - 4x + 13$

19) $-38x + 24$

20) $54x - 25$

21) $59x + 24$

22) $-x + 15$

23) $-3x^2 - 15x$

24) $-15x^2 + 22x$

25) $-40x^2 + 74x$

26) $2x^2 + 40x + 12$

27) $5x^2 - 15x - 10$

28) $2x^2 + 16x - 7$

29) $-8x^2 + 6x - 5$

30) $-3x^2 - 10x + 3$

31) $6x^2 + 15x + 18$

32) $6x^2 + 7x + 20$

Chapter 6: Expressions and Variables

Simplifying Polynomial Expressions

1) $3x^3 + x^2 - 10x$

2) $-4x^5 - 2x^3 - 5x^2$

3) $18x^4 + 5x^2$

4) $-15x^3 - 8x^2 + 6x$

5) $-7x^3 + 6x^2 - 3$

6) $2x^4 + 13x^3 - 8x$

7) $-15x^3 - 12x^2 + 8x$

8) $-2x^3 - 3x^2 - 2x$

9) $-4x^4 + 2x^3 + x^2 - 2x$

10) $x^4 - 9x^2 - 14x$

11) $3x^4 - 3x^2$

12) $15x^4 - 17x^3 + 4x^2$

13) $10x^4 - 10x^3 + 3x^2$

14) $6x^3 - 4x^2 + 14x$

15) $-6x^5 + 10x^4 - 9x^2$

16) $2x^3 - 4x^2 + 15x$

Evaluating One Variable

1) 0
2) 6
3) 32
4) 16
5) 8
6) 16
7) −3
8) 16
9) −1
10) 13
11) 6
12) −4
13) −68
14) −40
15) 9
16) 29
17) −27
18) −17
19) 22
20) 7
21) 33
22) 21
23) 20
24) 14
25) 34
26) 44

Chapter 6: Expressions and Variables

Evaluating Two Variables

1) 11
2) −21
3) −3
4) 3
5) 10
6) 4
7) 38
8) −30
9) 4
10) −6
11) −20
12) 42
13) 25
14) −19
15) 18
16) 30
17) 42
18) −9
19) −28
20) −9
21) −42
22) −44

The Distributive Property

1) $-20x - 6$
2) $15x - 25$
3) $-33x + 33$
4) $-24x + 30$
5) $20x - 24$
6) $-18x + 72$
7) $-20x + 30$
8) $16x - 56$
9) $-32x + 56$
10) $27x - 15$
11) $-8x + 72$
12) $-42x + 14$
13) $36x - 12$
14) $60x - 36$
15) $55x - 25$
16) $-72x + 36$
17) $-42x + 14$
18) $108x - 9$
19) $18x - 12$
20) $16x - 4$
21) $-20x + 40$
22) $-48x + 36$
23) $-48x + 36$
24) $-18x + 18$
25) $30x - 18$
26) $-91x + 52$

Chapter 7: Equations and Inequalities

Math Topics that you'll learn in this Chapter:

- ✓ One–Step Equations
- ✓ Multi–Step Equations
- ✓ System of Equations
- ✓ Graphing Single–Variable Inequalities
- ✓ One–Step Inequalities
- ✓ Multi–Step Inequalities

Chapter 7: Equations and Inequalities

One–Step Equations

✏️ *Solve each equation for x.*

1) $x - 18 = 28 \Rightarrow x =$ ____

2) $19 = -5 + x \Rightarrow x =$ ____

3) $15 - x = 6 \Rightarrow x =$ ____

4) $x - 24 = 29 \Rightarrow x =$ ____

5) $24 - x = 17 \Rightarrow x =$ ____

6) $16 - x = 3 \Rightarrow x =$ ____

7) $x + 14 = 12 \Rightarrow x =$ ____

8) $26 + x = 8 \Rightarrow x =$ ____

9) $x + 9 = -18 \Rightarrow x =$ ____

10) $x + 21 = 11 \Rightarrow x =$ ____

11) $17 = -5 + x \Rightarrow x =$ ____

12) $x + 20 = 29 \Rightarrow x =$ ____

13) $x - 13 = 19 \Rightarrow x =$ ____

14) $x + 9 = -17 \Rightarrow x =$ ____

15) $x + 4 = -23 \Rightarrow x =$ ____

16) $16 = -9 + x \Rightarrow x =$ ____

17) $4x = 28 \Rightarrow x =$ ____

18) $21 = -7x \Rightarrow x =$ ____

19) $12x = -12 \Rightarrow x =$ ____

20) $13x = 39 \Rightarrow x =$ ____

21) $8x = -16 \Rightarrow x =$ ____

22) $\frac{x}{2} = -5 \Rightarrow x =$ ____

23) $\frac{x}{9} = 6 \Rightarrow x =$ ____

24) $27 = \frac{x}{5} \Rightarrow x =$ ____

25) $\frac{x}{4} = -3 \Rightarrow x =$ ____

26) $x \div 8 = 7 \Rightarrow x =$ ____

27) $x \div 2 = -3 \Rightarrow x =$ ____

28) $8x = 56 \Rightarrow x =$ ____

29) $9x = 54 \Rightarrow x =$ ____

30) $7x = -35 \Rightarrow x =$ ____

31) $60 = -10x \Rightarrow x =$ ____

Chapter 7: Equations and Inequalities

Multi –Step Equations

✎ Solve each equation.

1) $4x - 7 = 13 \Rightarrow x =$ ____

2) $26 = -(x - 4) \Rightarrow x =$ ____

3) $-(5 - x) = 19 \Rightarrow x =$ ____

4) $35 = -x + 14 \Rightarrow x =$ ____

5) $2(3 - 2x) = 10 \Rightarrow x =$ ____

6) $3x - 3 = 15 \Rightarrow x =$ ____

7) $32 = -x + 15 \Rightarrow x =$ ____

8) $-(10 - x) = -13 \Rightarrow x =$ ____

9) $-4(7 + x) = 4 \Rightarrow x =$ ____

10) $22 = 2x - 8 \Rightarrow x =$ ____

11) $-6(3 + x) = 6 \Rightarrow x =$ ____

12) $-3 = 3x - 15 \Rightarrow x =$ ____

13) $-7(12 + x) = 7 \Rightarrow x =$ ____

14) $8(6 - 4x) = 16 \Rightarrow x =$ ____

15) $18 - 4x = -9 - x \Rightarrow x =$ ____

16) $6(4 - x) = 30 \Rightarrow x =$ ____

17) $15 - 3x = -5 - x \Rightarrow x =$ ____

18) $9(-7 - 3x) = 18 \Rightarrow x =$ ____

19) $16 - 2x = -4 - 7x \Rightarrow x =$ ____

20) $14 - 2x = 14 + x \Rightarrow x =$ ____

21) $21 - 3x = -7 - 10x \Rightarrow x =$ ____

22) $8 - 2x = 11 + x \Rightarrow x =$ ____

23) $10 + 12x = -8 + 6x \Rightarrow x =$ ____

24) $25 + 20x = -5 + 5x \Rightarrow x =$ ____

25) $16 - x = -8 - 7x \Rightarrow x =$ ____

26) $17 - 3x = 13 + x \Rightarrow x =$ ____

27) $22 + 5x = -8 - x \Rightarrow x =$ ____

28) $-9(7 + x) = 9 \Rightarrow x =$ ____

29) $12 + 2x = -4 - 2x \Rightarrow x =$ ____

30) $12 - x = 2 - 3x \Rightarrow x =$ ____

31) $19 - x = -1 - 11x \Rightarrow x =$ ____

32) $14 - 3x = -5 - 4x \Rightarrow x =$ ____

Chapter 7: Equations and Inequalities

System of Equations

✍ *Solve each system of equations.*

1) $2x + 3y = 15$ $x =$
   $x - 3y = 3$ $y =$

2) $y = x + 3$ $x =$
   $x + y = -5$ $y =$

3) $x + 3y = 6$ $x =$
   $2x + 8y = -12$ $y =$

4) $2x + y = 5$ $x =$
   $-3x + 6y = 0$ $y =$

5) $10x - 8y = -15$ $x =$
   $-6x + 4y = 13$ $y =$

6) $-3x - 4y = 5$ $x =$
   $x - 2y = 5$ $y =$

7) $5x - 12y = -19$ $x =$
   $-6x + 7y = 8$ $y =$

8) $5x - 7y = -2$ $x =$
   $-x - 2y = -3$ $y =$

9) $-x + 3y = 3$ $x =$
   $-7x + 8y = -5$ $y =$

10) $-4x + 3y = -18$ $x =$
    $4x - y = 14$ $y =$

11) $6x - 7y = -8$ $x =$
    $-x - 4y = -9$ $y =$

12) $-3x + 2y = -16$ $x =$
    $4x - y = 13$ $y =$

13) $2x + 3y = 8$ $x =$
    $-3x + 2y = 1$ $y =$

14) $y = -x + 3$ $x =$
    $3y + 5x = -1$ $y =$

15) $2x + 3y = 12$ $x =$
    $x + y = 5$ $y =$

16) $y = x - 1$ $x =$
    $y = 2x + 2$ $y =$

Chapter 7: Equations and Inequalities

Graphing Single–Variable Inequalities

✎ *Graph each inequality.*

1) $x < 5$

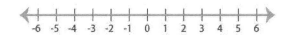

2) $x \geq 2$

3) $x \geq -4$

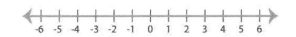

4) $x \leq -1$

5) $x > -1$

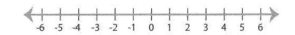

6) $3 > x$

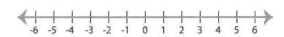

7) $2 \leq x$

8) $x > 0$

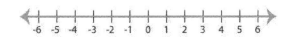

9) $-3 \leq x$

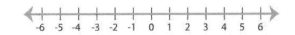

10) $-4 \leq x$

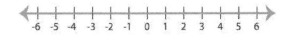

11) $x \leq 6$

12) $1 \leq x$

13) $-4 < x$

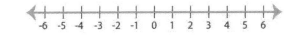

14) $x > -5$

Chapter 7: Equations and Inequalities

One–Step Inequalities

✏️ *Solve each inequality for* x.

1) $x - 9 < 20 \Rightarrow$ _____

2) $14 \leq -6 + x \Rightarrow$ _____

3) $x - 31 > 9 \Rightarrow$ _____

4) $x + 28 \geq 36 \Rightarrow$ _____

5) $x - 24 > 17 \Rightarrow$ _____

6) $x + 5 \geq 3 \Rightarrow x$ _____

7) $x + 14 < 12 \Rightarrow$ _____

8) $26 + x \leq 8 \Rightarrow$ _____

9) $x + 9 \geq -18 \Rightarrow$ _____

10) $x + 24 < 11 \Rightarrow$ _____

11) $17 \leq -5 + x \Rightarrow$ _____

12) $x + 25 > 29 \Rightarrow x$ _____

13) $x - 17 \geq 19 \Rightarrow$ _____

14) $x + 8 > -17 \Rightarrow$ _____

15) $x + 8 < -23 \Rightarrow$ _____

16) $16 \leq -5 + x \Rightarrow$ _____

17) $4x \leq 12 \Rightarrow$ _____

18) $28 \geq -7x \Rightarrow$ _____

19) $2x > -14 \Rightarrow$ _____

20) $13x \leq 39 \Rightarrow$ _____

21) $-8x > -16 \Rightarrow$ _____

22) $\frac{x}{2} < -6 \Rightarrow$ _____

23) $\frac{x}{6} > 6 \Rightarrow$ _____

24) $27 \leq \frac{x}{4} \Rightarrow$ _____

25) $\frac{x}{8} < -3 \Rightarrow$ _____

26) $6x \geq 18 \Rightarrow$ _____

27) $5x \geq -25 \Rightarrow$ _____

28) $3x > 45 \Rightarrow$ _____

29) $9x \leq 72 \Rightarrow$ _____

30) $-6x < -36 \Rightarrow$ _____

31) $70 > -10x \Rightarrow$ _____

Chapter 7: Equations and Inequalities

Multi –Step Inequalities

✍ *Solve each inequality.*

1) $2x - 6 \leq 4 \rightarrow$ _____

2) $2 + 3x \geq 17 \rightarrow$ _____

3) $9 + 3x \geq 36 \rightarrow$ _____

4) $2x - 6 \leq 18 \rightarrow$ _____

5) $3x - 4 \leq 23 \rightarrow$ _____

6) $7x - 5 \leq 51 \rightarrow$ _____

7) $4x - 9 \leq 27 \rightarrow$ _____

8) $6x - 11 \leq 13 \rightarrow$ _____

9) $5x - 7 \leq 33 \rightarrow$ _____

10) $6 + 2x \geq 28 \rightarrow$ _____

11) $8 + 3x \geq 35 \rightarrow$ _____

12) $4 + 6x < 34 \rightarrow$ _____

13) $3 + 2x \geq 53 \rightarrow$ _____

14) $7 - 6x > 56 + x \rightarrow$ _____

15) $9 + 4x \geq 39 + 2x \rightarrow$ _____

16) $3 + 5x \geq 43 \rightarrow$ _____

17) $4 - 7x < 60 \rightarrow$ _____

18) $11 - 4x \geq 55 \rightarrow$ _____

19) $12 + x \geq 48 - 2x \rightarrow$ _____

20) $10 - 10x \leq -20 \rightarrow$ _____

21) $5 - 9x \geq -40 \rightarrow$ _____

22) $8 - 7x \geq 36 \rightarrow$ _____

23) $6 + 10x < 69 + 3x \rightarrow$ _____

24) $5 + 4x < 26 - 3x \rightarrow$ _____

25) $10 + 11x < 59 + 4x \rightarrow$ _____

26) $3 + 9x \geq 48 - 6x \rightarrow$ _____

Chapter 7: Equations and Inequalities

Answers – Chapter 7

One–Step Equations

1) $x = 46$
2) $x = 24$
3) $x = 9$
4) $x = 53$
5) $x = 7$
6) $x = 13$
7) $x = -2$
8) $x = -18$
9) $x = -27$
10) $x = -10$
11) $x = 22$
12) $x = 9$
13) $x = 32$
14) $x = -26$
15) $x = -27$
16) $x = 25$
17) $x = 7$
18) $x = -3$
19) $x = -1$
20) $x = 3$
21) $x = -2$
22) $x = -10$
23) $x = 54$
24) $x = 135$
25) $x = -12$
26) $x = 56$
27) $x = -6$
28) $x = 7$
29) $x = 6$
30) $x = -5$
31) $x = -6$

Multi –Step Equations

1) $x = 5$
2) $x = -22$
3) $x = 24$
4) $x = -21$
5) $x = -1$
6) $x = 6$
7) $x = -17$
8) $x = -3$
9) $x = -8$
10) $x = 15$
11) $x = -4$
12) $x = 4$
13) $x = -13$
14) $x = 1$
15) $x = 9$
16) $x = -1$
17) $x = 10$
18) $x = -3$
19) $x = -4$
20) $x = 0$
21) $x = -4$
22) $x = -1$
23) $x = -3$
24) $x = -2$
25) $x = -4$
26) $x = 1$
27) $x = -5$
28) $x = -8$
29) $x = -4$
30) $x = -5$
31) $x = -2$
32) $x = -19$

Chapter 7: Equations and Inequalities

System of Equations

1) $x = 6, y = 1$

2) $x = -4, y = -1$

3) $x = 42, y = -12$

4) $x = 2, y = 1$

5) $x = -\frac{11}{2}, y = -5$

6) $x = 1, y = -2$

7) $x = 1, y = 2$

8) $x = 1, y = 1$

9) $x = 3, y = 2$

10) $x = 3, y = -2$

11) $x = 1, y = 2$

12) $x = 2, y = -5$

13) $x = 1, y = 2$

14) $x = -5, y = 8$

15) $x = 3, y = 2$

16) $x = -3, y = -4$

Chapter 7: Equations and Inequalities

Graphing Single–Variable Inequalities

1) $x < 5$

2) $x \geq 2$

3) $x \geq -4$
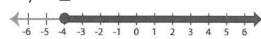

4) $x \leq -1$

5) $x > -1$

6) $3 > x$

7) $2 \leq x$

8) $x > 0$

9) $-3 \leq x$

10) $-4 \leq x$

11) $x \leq 6$

12) $1 \leq x$
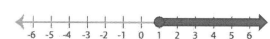

13) $-4 < x$
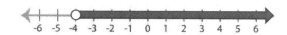

14) $x > -5$

Chapter 7: Equations and Inequalities

One–Step Inequalities

1) $x < 29$
2) $20 \leq x$
3) $x > 40$
4) $x \geq 8$
5) $x > 41$
6) $x \geq -2$
7) $x < -2$
8) $x \leq -18$
9) $x \geq -27$
10) $x < -13$
11) $22 \leq x$
12) $x > 4$
13) $x \geq 36$
14) $x > -25$
15) $x < -31$
16) $21 \leq x$
17) $x \leq 3$
18) $-4 \leq x$
19) $x > -7$
20) $x \leq 3$
21) $x < 2$
22) $x < -12$
23) $x > 36$
24) $108 \leq x$
25) $x < -24$
26) $x \geq 3$
27) $x \geq -5$
28) $x > 15$
29) $x \leq 8$
30) $x > 6$
31) $-7 < x$

Multi–Step Inequalities

1) $x \leq 5$
2) $x \geq 5$
3) $x \geq 9$
4) $x \leq 12$
5) $x \leq 9$
6) $x \leq 8$
7) $x \leq 9$
8) $x \leq 4$
9) $x \leq 8$
10) $x \geq 11$
11) $x \geq 9$
12) $x < 5$
13) $x \geq 25$
14) $x < -7$
15) $x \geq 15$
16) $x \geq 8$
17) $x > -8$
18) $x \leq -11$
19) $x \geq 12$
20) $x \geq 3$
21) $x \leq 5$
22) $x \leq -4$
23) $x < 9$
24) $x < 3$
25) $x < 7$
26) $x \geq 3$

Chapter 8: Lines and Slope

Math Topics that you'll learn in this Chapter:

- ✓ Finding Slope
- ✓ Graphing Lines Using Slope–Intercept Form
- ✓ Writing Linear Equations
- ✓ Graphing Linear Inequalities
- ✓ Finding Midpoint
- ✓ Finding Distance of Two Points

Chapter 8: Lines and Slope

Finding Slope

✎ **Find the slope of each line.**

1) $y = 2x - 8$, Slope =

2) $y = -6x + 3$, Slope =

3) $y = -x - 5$, Slope =

4) $y = -2x - 9$, Slope =

5) $y = 5 + 2x$, Slope =

6) $y = 1 - 8x$, Slope =

7) $y = -4x + 3$, Slope =

8) $y = -9x + 8$, Slope =

9) $y = -2x + 4$, Slope =

10) $y = 9x - 8$, Slope =

11) $y = \frac{1}{2}x + 4$, Slope =

12) $y = -\frac{2}{5}x + 7$, Slope =

13) $-x + 3y = 5$, Slope =

14) $4x + 4y = 6$, Slope =

15) $6y - 2x = 10$, Slope =

16) $3y - x = 2$, Slope =

✎ **Find the slope of the line through each pair of points.**

17) $(4, 4), (8, 12)$, Slope =

23) $(8, 4), (9, 6)$, Slope =

18) $(-2, 4), (0, 6)$, Slope =

24) $(10, -1), (7, 8)$, Slope =

19) $(6, -2), (2, 6)$, Slope =

25) $(16, -3), (13, -6)$, Slope =

20) $(-4, -2), (0, 6)$, Slope =

26) $(12, 5), (8, 1)$, Slope =

21) $(6, 2), (3, 5)$, Slope =

27) $(6, 6), (8, 10)$, Slope =

22) $(-5, 1), (-1, 9)$, Slope =

28) $(10, -1), (8, 1)$, Slope =

Chapter 8: Lines and Slope

Graphing Lines Using Slope–Intercept Form

✏️ *Sketch the graph of each line.*

1) $y = -x + 1$

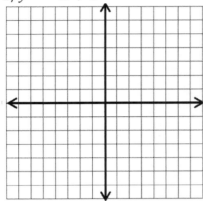

2) $y = 2x - 4$

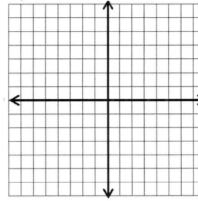

3) $y = -x + 6$

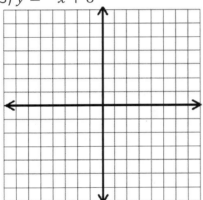

4) $y = x - 4$

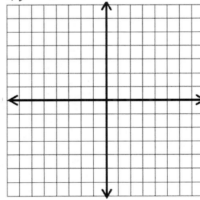

5) $y = 2x - 2$

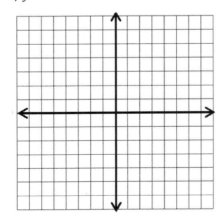

6) $y = -\frac{1}{2}x + 2$

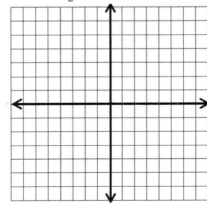

Chapter 8: Lines and Slope

Writing Linear Equations

Write the equation of the line through the given points.

1) through: $(2, -2), (3, 4)$ $y =$

2) through: $(-2, 4), (1, 7)$ $y =$

3) through: $(-1, 3), (3, 7)$ $y =$

4) through: $(6, 5), (3, 2)$ $y =$

5) through: $(7, -10), (2, 10)$ $y =$

6) through: $(7, 2), (6, 1)$ $y =$

7) through: $(6, -1), (4, 1)$ $y =$

8) through: $(-2, 8), (-4, -6)$ $y =$

9) through: $(-2, 5), (-3, 4)$ $y =$

10) through: $(6, 8), (8, -6)$ $y =$

11) through: $(-2, 5), (-4, -3)$ $y =$

12) through: $(8, 8), (4, -8)$ $y =$

13) through: $(7, -4)$, Slope: -1 $y =$

14) through: $(4, -10)$, Slope: -2 $y =$

15) through: $(6, 10)$, Slope: 9 $y =$

16) through: $(-6, 8)$, Slope: -2 $y =$

Solve each problem.

17) What is the equation of a line with slope 6 and intercept 4? _____

18) What is the equation of a line with slope 5 and intercept 9? _____

19) What is the equation of a line with slope 8 and passes through point $(2, 8)$? _____

20) What is the equation of a line with slope -3 and passes through point $(-4, 10)$? _____

Chapter 8: Lines and Slope

Finding Midpoint

✏️ *Find the midpoint of the line segment with the given endpoints.*

1) $(4, 4), (0, 4)$,   midpoint = (__, __)
2) $(5, 1), (-1, 5)$,   midpoint = (__, __)
3) $(4, -2), (0, 6)$,   midpoint = (__, __)
4) $(-3, 3), (-1, 5)$,   midpoint = (__, __)
5) $(5, -2), (9, -6)$,   midpoint = (__, __)
6) $(-6, -3), (4, -7)$,   midpoint = (__, __)
7) $(7, 0), (-7, 8)$,   midpoint = (__, __)
8) $(-8, 4), (-4, 0)$,   midpoint = (__, __)
9) $(-3, 6), (9, -8)$,   midpoint = (__, __)
10) $(6, 8), (6, -6)$,   midpoint = (__, __)
11) $(6, 7), (-8, 5)$,   midpoint = (__, __)
12) $(9, 3), (-3, -9)$,   midpoint = (__, __)
13) $(-6, 12), (-4, 6)$,   midpoint = (__, __)
14) $(10, 7), (8, -3)$,   midpoint = (__, __)
15) $(13, 7), (-5, 3)$,   midpoint = (__, __)
16) $(-9, -4), (-5, 8)$,   midpoint = (__, __)
17) $(12, 5), (6, 15)$,   midpoint = (__, __)
18) $(-6, -10), (12, -2)$,   midpoint = (__, __)
19) $(14, 13), (-4, 9)$,   midpoint = (__, __)
20) $(10, -4), (8, 12)$,   midpoint = (__, __)

Chapter 8: Lines and Slope

Finding Distance of Two Points

✎ **Find the distance of each pair of points.**

1) $(0, 9), (4, 6)$,

    Distance = ____

2) $(-4, 6), (8, 11)$,

    Distance = ____

3) $(-6, 1), (-3, 5)$,

    Distance = ____

4) $(-3, 2), (3, 10)$,

    Distance = ____

5) $(-5, 3), (4, -9)$,

    Distance = ____

6) $(-7, -5), (5, 0)$,

    Distance = ____

7) $(4, 3), (-4, -12)$,

    Distance = ____

8) $(10, 1), (-5, -19)$,

    Distance = ____

9) $(3, 3), (-1, 5)$,

    Distance = ____

10) $(2, -1), (10, 5)$,

    Distance = ____

11) $(-3, 7), (-1, 4)$,

    Distance = ____

12) $(5, -2), (9, -5)$,

    Distance = ____

13) $(-8, 4), (4, 9)$,

    Distance = ____

14) $(6, 8), (6, -6)$,

    Distance = ____

15) $(6, -6), (0, 2)$,

    Distance = ____

16) $(-4, 10), (-4, 4)$,

    Distance = ____

17) $(-7, -6), (-2, 6)$,

    Distance = ____

18) $(11, 0), (3, 15)$,

    Distance = ____

Chapter 8: Lines and Slope

Answers – Chapter 8

Finding Slope

1) 2
2) −6
3) −1
4) −2
5) 2
6) −8
7) −4
8) −9
9) −2
10) 9
11) $\frac{1}{2}$
12) $-\frac{2}{5}$
13) $\frac{1}{3}$
14) −1
15) $\frac{1}{3}$
16) $\frac{1}{3}$
17) 2
18) 1
19) −2
20) 2
21) −1
22) 2
23) 2
24) −3
25) 1
26) 1
27) 2
28) −1

Graphing Lines Using Slope–Intercept Form

1) $y = -x + 1$
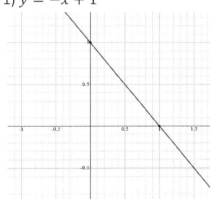

2) $y = 2x - 4$
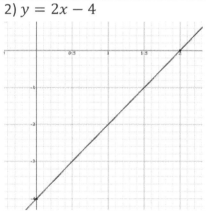

3) $y = -x + 6$
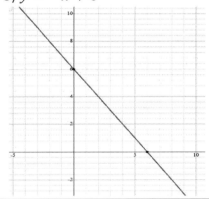

4) $y = x - 4$
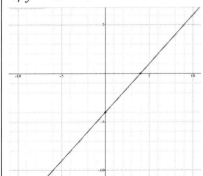

5) $y = 2x - 2$
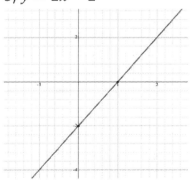

6) $y = -\frac{1}{2}x + 2$
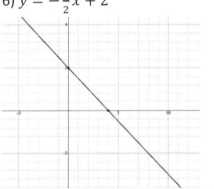

Chapter 8: Lines and Slope

Writing Linear Equations

1) $y = 6x - 14$
2) $y = x + 6$
3) $y = x + 4$
4) $y = x - 1$
5) $y = -4x + 18$
6) $y = x - 5$
7) $y = -x + 5$
8) $y = 7x + 22$
9) $y = x + 7$
10) $y = -7x + 50$
11) $y = 4x + 13$
12) $y = 4x - 24$
13) $y = -x + 3$
14) $y = -2x - 2$
15) $y = 9x - 44$
16) $y = -2x - 4$
17) $y = 6x + 4$
18) $y = 5x + 9$
19) $y = 8x - 8$
20) $y = -3x - 2$

Finding Midpoint

1) $midpoint = (2, 4)$
2) $midpoint = (2, 3)$
3) $midpoint = (2, 2)$
4) $midpoint = (-2, 4)$
5) $midpoint = (7, -4)$
6) $midpoint = (-1, -5)$
7) $midpoint = (0, 4)$
8) $midpoint = (-6, 2)$
9) $midpoint = (3, -1)$
10) $midpoint = (6, 1)$
11) $midpoint = (-1, 6)$
12) $midpoint = (3, -3)$
13) $midpoint = (-5, 9)$
14) $midpoint = (9, 2)$
15) $midpoint = (4, 5)$
16) $midpoint = (-7, 2)$
17) $midpoint = (9, 10)$
18) $midpoint = (3, -6)$
19) $midpoint = (5, 11)$
20) $midpoint = (9, 4)$

Chapter 8: Lines and Slope

Finding Distance of Two Points

1) Distance = 5

2) Distance = 13

3) Distance = 5

4) Distance = 10

5) Distance = 15

6) Distance = 13

7) Distance = 17

8) Distance = 25

9) Distance = $\sqrt{20} = 2\sqrt{5}$

10) Distance = 10

11) Distance = $\sqrt{13}$

12) Distance = 5

13) Distance = 13

14) Distance = 14

15) Distance = 10

16) Distance = 6

17) Distance = 13

18) Distance = 17

Chapter 9: Exponents and Variables

Math Topics that you'll learn in this Chapter:

- ✓ Multiplication Property of Exponents
- ✓ Division Property of Exponents
- ✓ Powers of Products and Quotients
- ✓ Zero and Negative Exponents
- ✓ Negative Exponents and Negative Bases
- ✓ Scientific Notation
- ✓ Radicals

Chapter 9: Exponents and Variables

Multiplication Property of Exponents

✎ *Simplify and write the answer in exponential form.*

1) $3 \times 3^2 =$

2) $4^3 \times 4 =$

3) $2^2 \times 2^2 =$

4) $6^2 \times 6^2 =$

5) $7^3 \times 7^2 \times 7 =$

6) $2 \times 2^2 \times 2^2 =$

7) $5^3 \times 5^2 \times 5 \times 5 =$

8) $2x \times x =$

9) $x^3 \times x^2 =$

10) $x^4 \times x^4 =$

11) $x^2 \times x^2 \times x^2 =$

12) $6x \times 6x =$

13) $2x^2 \times 2x^2 =$

14) $3x^2 \times x =$

15) $4x^4 \times 4x^4 \times 4x^4 =$

16) $2x^2 \times x^2 =$

17) $x^4 \times 3x =$

18) $x \times 2x^2 =$

19) $5x^4 \times 5x^4 =$

20) $2yx^2 \times 2x =$

21) $3x^4 \times y^2x^4 =$

22) $y^2x^3 \times y^5x^2 =$

23) $4yx^3 \times 2x^2y^3 =$

24) $6x^2 \times 6x^3y^4 =$

25) $3x^4y^5 \times 7x^2y^3 =$

26) $7x^2y^5 \times 9xy^3 =$

27) $7xy^4 \times 4x^3y^3 =$

28) $3x^5y^3 \times 8x^2y^3 =$

29) $6x \times y^5x^2 \times y^3 =$

30) $yx^3 \times 3y^3x^2 \times 2xy =$

31) $5yx^3 \times 4y^2x \times xy^3 =$

32) $6x^2 \times 3x^3y^4 \times 10yx^3 =$

Chapter 9: Exponents and Variables

Division Property of Exponents

✎ *Simplify and write the answer.*

1) $\dfrac{3^2}{3^3} =$

2) $\dfrac{2^6}{2^2} =$

3) $\dfrac{4^4}{4} =$

4) $\dfrac{5}{5^4} =$

5) $\dfrac{x}{x^3} =$

6) $\dfrac{3 \times 3^3}{3^2 \times 3^4} =$

7) $\dfrac{5^8}{5^3} =$

8) $\dfrac{5 \times 5^6}{5^2 \times 5^7} =$

9) $\dfrac{3^4 \times 3^7}{3^2 \times 3^8} =$

10) $\dfrac{5x}{10x^3} =$

11) $\dfrac{5x^3}{2x^5} =$

12) $\dfrac{18x^3}{14x^6} =$

13) $\dfrac{12x^3}{8xy^8} =$

14) $\dfrac{24xy^3}{4x^4y^2} =$

15) $\dfrac{21x^3y^9}{7xy^5} =$

16) $\dfrac{36x^2y^9}{4x^3} =$

17) $\dfrac{18x^3y^4}{10x^6y^8} =$

18) $\dfrac{16y^2x^{14}}{24yx^8} =$

19) $\dfrac{15x^4y}{9x^9y^2} =$

20) $\dfrac{7x^7y^2}{28x^5y^6} =$

Chapter 9: Exponents and Variables

Powers of Products and Quotients

✎ *Simplify and write the answer.*

1) $(3^2)^2 =$

2) $(5^2)^3 =$

3) $(3 \times 3^3)^4 =$

4) $(6 \times 6^4)^2 =$

5) $(3^3 \times 3^2)^3 =$

6) $(5^4 \times 5^5)^2 =$

7) $(2 \times 2^4)^2 =$

8) $(2x^6)^2 =$

9) $(11x^5)^2 =$

10) $(4x^2y^4)^4 =$

11) $(2x^4y^4)^3 =$

12) $(3x^2y^2)^2 =$

13) $(3x^4y^3)^4 =$

14) $(2x^6y^8)^2 =$

15) $(12x^3x)^3 =$

16) $(5x^9x^6)^3 =$

17) $(5x^{10}y^3)^3 =$

18) $(14x^3x^3)^2 =$

19) $(3x^35x)^2 =$

20) $(10x^{11}y^3)^2 =$

21) $(9x^7y^5)^2 =$

22) $(4x^4y^6)^5 =$

23) $(3x4y^3)^2 =$

24) $\left(\dfrac{6x}{x^2}\right)^2 =$

25) $\left(\dfrac{x^5y^5}{x^2y^2}\right)^3 =$

26) $\left(\dfrac{24x}{4x^6}\right)^2 =$

27) $\left(\dfrac{x^5}{x^6y^2}\right)^2 =$

28) $\left(\dfrac{xy^3}{x^2y^5}\right)^3 =$

29) $\left(\dfrac{3xy^3}{x^4}\right)^2 =$

30) $\left(\dfrac{xy^5}{4xy^3}\right)^3 =$

Chapter 9: Exponents and Variables

Zero and Negative Exponents

✎ *Evaluate the following expressions.*

1) $2^{-1} =$

2) $3^{-2} =$

3) $0^{10} =$

4) $1^{-8} =$

5) $8^{-1} =$

6) $8^{-2} =$

7) $2^{-4} =$

8) $10^{-2} =$

9) $9^{-2} =$

10) $3^{-3} =$

11) $7^{-3} =$

12) $3^{-4} =$

13) $6^{-3} =$

14) $5^{-3} =$

15) $22^{-1} =$

16) $4^{-4} =$

17) $5^{-4} =$

18) $15^{-2} =$

19) $4^{-5} =$

20) $9^{-3} =$

21) $3^{-5} =$

22) $5^{-4} =$

23) $12^{-2} =$

24) $15^{-3} =$

25) $20^{-3} =$

26) $50^{-2} =$

27) $18^{-3} =$

28) $24^{-2} =$

29) $30^{-3} =$

30) $10^{-5} =$

31) $\left(\frac{1}{8}\right)^{-1} =$

32) $\left(\frac{1}{5}\right)^{-2} =$

33) $\left(\frac{1}{7}\right)^{-2} =$

34) $\left(\frac{2}{3}\right)^{-2} =$

35) $\left(\frac{1}{5}\right)^{-3} =$

36) $\left(\frac{3}{4}\right)^{-2} =$

37) $\left(\frac{2}{5}\right)^{-2} =$

38) $\left(\frac{1}{2}\right)^{-8} =$

39) $\left(\frac{2}{3}\right)^{-3} =$

40) $\left(\frac{3}{4}\right)^{-3} =$

41) $\left(\frac{5}{6}\right)^{-2} =$

42) $\left(\frac{6}{9}\right)^{-2} =$

Chapter 9: Exponents and Variables

Negative Exponents and Negative Bases

✏️ *Simplify and write the answer.*

1) $-2^{-1} =$

2) $-4^{-2} =$

3) $-3^{-4} =$

4) $-x^{-5} =$

5) $2x^{-1} =$

6) $-4x^{-3} =$

7) $-12x^{-5} =$

8) $-5x^{-2}y^{-3} =$

9) $20x^{-4}y^{-1} =$

10) $14a^{-6}b^{-7} =$

11) $-12x^2y^{-3} =$

12) $-\dfrac{25}{x^{-6}} =$

13) $-\dfrac{2x}{y^{-4}} =$

14) $\left(-\dfrac{1}{3x}\right)^{-2} =$

15) $\left(-\dfrac{3}{4x}\right)^{-2} =$

16) $-\dfrac{9}{a^{-7}b^{-2}} =$

17) $-\dfrac{5x}{x^{-3}} =$

18) $-\dfrac{a^{-3}}{b^{-2}} =$

19) $-\dfrac{8}{x^{-3}} =$

20) $\dfrac{5b}{-9c^{-4}} =$

21) $\dfrac{9ab}{a^{-3}b^{-1}} =$

22) $-\dfrac{15a^{-2}}{30b^{-3}} =$

23) $\dfrac{4ab^{-2}}{-3c^{-2}} =$

24) $\left(\dfrac{3a}{2c}\right)^{-2} =$

25) $\left(-\dfrac{3x}{4yz}\right)^{-2} =$

26) $\dfrac{15ab^{-6}}{-9c^{-2}} =$

27) $\left(-\dfrac{x^3}{x^4}\right)^{-3} =$

28) $\left(-\dfrac{x^{-2}}{2x^2}\right)^{-2} =$

Chapter 9: Exponents and Variables

Scientific Notation

✎ *Write each number in scientific notation.*

1) $0.114 =$

2) $0.06 =$

3) $8.6 =$

4) $30 =$

5) $60 =$

6) $0.004 =$

7) $78 =$

8) $1,600 =$

9) $1,450 =$

10) $31,000 =$

11) $2,000,000 =$

12) $0.0000003 =$

13) $554,000 =$

14) $0.000725 =$

15) $0.00034 =$

16) $86,000,000 =$

17) $62,000 =$

18) $97,000,000 =$

19) $0.0000045 =$

20) $0.0019 =$

✎ *Write each number in standard notation.*

21) $2 \times 10^{-1} =$

22) $8 \times 10^{-2} =$

23) $1.8 \times 10^3 =$

24) $9 \times 10^{-4} =$

25) $1.7 \times 10^{-2} =$

26) $9 \times 10^3 =$

27) $6 \times 10^4 =$

28) $2.18 \times 10^5 =$

29) $5 \times 10^{-3} =$

30) $9.4 \times 10^{-5} =$

Chapter 9: Exponents and Variables

Radicals

✎ *Simplify and write the answer.*

1) $\sqrt{1} =$ ____

2) $\sqrt{0} =$ ____

3) $\sqrt{16} =$ ____

4) $\sqrt{4} =$ ____

5) $\sqrt{9} =$ ____

6) $\sqrt{25} =$ ____

7) $\sqrt{49} =$ ____

8) $\sqrt{36} =$ ____

9) $\sqrt{64} =$ ____

10) $\sqrt{81} =$ ____

11) $\sqrt{121} =$ ____

12) $\sqrt{225} =$ ____

13) $\sqrt{144} =$ ____

14) $\sqrt{100} =$ ____

15) $\sqrt{256} =$ ____

16) $\sqrt{289} =$ ____

17) $\sqrt{324} =$ ____

18) $\sqrt{400} =$ ____

19) $\sqrt{900} =$ ____

20) $\sqrt{529} =$ ____

21) $\sqrt{361} =$ ____

22) $\sqrt{169} =$ ____

23) $\sqrt{196} =$ ____

24) $\sqrt{90} =$ ____

✎ *Evaluate.*

25) $\sqrt{6} \times \sqrt{6} =$

26) $\sqrt{5} \times \sqrt{5} =$

27) $\sqrt{8} \times \sqrt{8} =$

28) $\sqrt{2} + \sqrt{2} =$

29) $\sqrt{8} + \sqrt{8} =$

30) $6\sqrt{5} - 2\sqrt{5} =$

31) $\sqrt{25} \times \sqrt{16} =$

32) $\sqrt{25} \times \sqrt{64} =$

33) $\sqrt{64} \times \sqrt{49} =$

34) $5\sqrt{5} \times 3\sqrt{5} =$

35) $7\sqrt{3} \times 2\sqrt{3} =$

36) $5\sqrt{2} - \sqrt{8} =$

Chapter 9: Exponents and Variables

Answers – Chapter 9

Multiplication Property of Exponents

1) 3^3
2) 4^4
3) 2^4
4) 6^4
5) 7^6
6) 2^5
7) 5^7
8) $2x^2$
9) x^5
10) x^8
11) x^6
12) $36x^2$
13) $4x^4$
14) $3x^3$
15) $64x^{12}$
16) $2x^4$
17) $3x^5$
18) $2x^3$
19) $25x^8$
20) $4x^3y$
21) $3x^8y^2$
22) x^5y^7
23) $8x^5y^4$
24) $36x^5y^4$
25) $21x^6y^8$
26) $63x^3y^8$
27) $28x^4y^7$
28) $24x^7y^6$
29) $6x^3y^8$
30) $6x^6y^5$
31) $20x^5y^6$
32) $180x^8y^5$

Division Property of Exponents

1) $\frac{1}{3}$
2) 2^4
3) 4^3
4) $\frac{1}{5^3}$
5) $\frac{1}{x^2}$
6) $\frac{1}{3^2}$
7) 5^5
8) $\frac{1}{5^2}$
9) 3
10) $\frac{1}{2x^2}$
11) $\frac{5}{2x^2}$
12) $\frac{9}{7x^3}$
13) $\frac{3x^2}{2y^8}$
14) $\frac{6y}{x^3}$
15) $3x^2y^4$
16) $\frac{9y^9}{x}$
17) $\frac{9}{5x^3y^4}$
18) $\frac{2yx^6}{3}$
19) $\frac{5}{3x^5y}$
20) $\frac{x^2}{4y^4}$

Chapter 9: Exponents and Variables

Powers of Products and Quotients

1) 3^4
2) 5^6
3) 3^{16}
4) 6^{10}
5) 3^{15}
6) 5^{18}
7) 2^{10}
8) $4x^{12}$
9) $121x^{10}$
10) $256x^8y^{16}$
11) $8x^{12}y^{12}$
12) $9x^4y^4$
13) $81x^{16}y^{12}$
14) $4x^{12}y^{16}$
15) $1,728x^{12}$
16) $125x^{45}$
17) $125x^{30}y^9$
18) $196x^{12}$
19) $225x^8$
20) $100x^{22}y^6$
21) $81x^{14}y^{10}$
22) $1,024x^{20}y^{30}$
23) $144x^2y^6$
24) $\dfrac{36}{x^2}$
25) x^9y^9
26) $\dfrac{36}{x^{10}}$
27) $\dfrac{1}{x^2y^4}$
28) $\dfrac{1}{x^3y^6}$
29) $\dfrac{9y^6}{x^6}$
30) $\dfrac{y^6}{64}$

Chapter 9: Exponents and Variables

Zero and Negative Exponents

1) $\frac{1}{2}$

2) $\frac{1}{9}$

3) 0

4) 1

5) $\frac{1}{8}$

6) $\frac{1}{64}$

7) $\frac{1}{16}$

8) $\frac{1}{100}$

9) $\frac{1}{81}$

10) $\frac{1}{27}$

11) $\frac{1}{343}$

12) $\frac{1}{81}$

13) $\frac{1}{216}$

14) $\frac{1}{125}$

15) $\frac{1}{22}$

16) $\frac{1}{256}$

17) $\frac{1}{625}$

18) $\frac{1}{225}$

19) $\frac{1}{1,024}$

20) $\frac{1}{729}$

21) $\frac{1}{243}$

22) $\frac{1}{625}$

23) $\frac{1}{144}$

24) $\frac{1}{3,375}$

25) $\frac{1}{8,000}$

26) $\frac{1}{2,500}$

27) $\frac{1}{5,832}$

28) $\frac{1}{576}$

29) $\frac{1}{27,000}$

30) $\frac{1}{100,000}$

31) 8

32) 25

33) 49

34) $\frac{9}{4}$

35) 125

36) $\frac{16}{9}$

37) $\frac{25}{4}$

38) 256

39) $\frac{27}{8}$

40) $\frac{64}{27}$

41) $\frac{36}{25}$

42) $\frac{81}{36}$

Chapter 9: Exponents and Variables

Negative Exponents and Negative Bases

1) $-\frac{1}{2}$

2) $-\frac{1}{16}$

3) $-\frac{1}{81}$

4) $-\frac{1}{x^5}$

5) $\frac{2}{x}$

6) $-\frac{4}{x^3}$

7) $-\frac{12}{x^5}$

8) $-\frac{5}{x^2y^3}$

9) $\frac{20}{x^4y}$

10) $\frac{14}{a^6b^7}$

11) $-\frac{12x^2}{y^3}$

12) $-25x^6$

13) $-2xy^4$

14) $9x^2$

15) $\frac{16x^2}{9}$

16) $-9a^7b^2$

17) $-5x^4$

18) $-\frac{b^2}{a^3}$

19) $-8x^3$

20) $-\frac{5bc^4}{9}$

21) $9a^4b^2$

22) $-\frac{b^3}{2a^2}$

23) $-\frac{4ac^2}{3b^2}$

24) $\frac{4c^2}{9a^2}$

25) $\frac{16y^2z^2}{9x^2}$

26) $-\frac{5ac^2}{3b^6}$

27) $-x^3$

28) $4x^8$

Chapter 9: Exponents and Variables

Scientific Notation

1) 1.14×10^{-1}
2) 6×10^{-2}
3) 8.6×10^{0}
4) 3×10^{1}
5) 6×10^{1}
6) 4×10^{-3}
7) 7.8×10^{1}
8) 1.6×10^{3}
9) 1.45×10^{3}
10) 3.1×10^{4}
11) 2×10^{6}
12) 3×10^{-7}
13) 5.54×10^{5}
14) 7.25×10^{-4}
15) 3.4×10^{-4}

16) 8.6×10^{7}
17) 6.2×10^{4}
18) 9.7×10^{7}
19) 4.5×10^{-6}
20) 1.9×10^{-3}
21) 0.2
22) 0.08
23) $1,800$
24) 0.0009
25) 0.017
26) $9,000$
27) $60,000$
28) $218,000$
29) 0.005
30) 0.000094

Chapter 9: Exponents and Variables

Radicals

1) 1
2) 0
3) 4
4) 2
5) 3
6) 5
7) 7
8) 6
9) 8
10) 9
11) 11
12) 15
13) 12
14) 10
15) 16
16) 17
17) 18
18) 20
19) 30
20) 23
21) 19
22) 13
23) 14
24) $3\sqrt{10}$
25) 6
26) 5
27) 8
28) $2\sqrt{2}$
29) $2\sqrt{8} = 4\sqrt{2}$
30) $4\sqrt{5}$
31) 20
32) 40
33) 56
34) 75
35) 42
36) $3\sqrt{2}$

Chapter 10: Polynomials

Math Topics that you'll learn in this Chapter:

- ✓ Simplifying Polynomials
- ✓ Adding and Subtracting Polynomials
- ✓ Multiplying Monomials
- ✓ Multiplying and Dividing Monomials
- ✓ Multiplying a Polynomial and a Monomial
- ✓ Multiplying Binomials
- ✓ Factoring Trinomials

Chapter 10: Polynomials

Simplifying Polynomials

Simplify each expression.

1) $3(2x + 1) =$ _____
2) $2(4x - 6) =$ _____
3) $4(3x + 3) =$ _____
4) $2(4x + 5) =$ _____
5) $-3(8x - 7) =$ _____
6) $2x(3x + 4) =$ _____
7) $3x^2 + 3x^2 - 2x^3 =$ _____
8) $2x - x^2 + 6x^3 + 4 =$ _____
9) $5x + 2x^2 - 9x^3 =$ _____
10) $7x^2 + 5x^4 - 2x^3 =$ _____
11) $-3x^2 + 5x^3 + 6x^4 =$ _____
12) $(x - 3)(x - 4) =$ _____
13) $(x - 5)(x + 4) =$ _____
14) $(x - 6)(x - 3) =$ _____
15) $(2x + 5)(x + 8) =$ _____
16) $(3x - 8)(x + 4) =$ _____
17) $-8x^2 + 2x^3 - 10x^4 + 5x =$ _____
18) $11 - 6x^2 + 5x^2 - 12x^3 + 22 =$ _____
19) $3x^2 - 4x + 4x^3 + 10x - 21x =$ _____
20) $10 - 6x^2 + 5x^2 - 3x^3 + 2 =$ _____
21) $3x^5 - 2x^3 + 8x^2 - x^5 =$ _____
22) $(5x^3 - 1) + (4x^3 - 6x^3) =$ _____

Chapter 10: Polynomials

Adding and Subtracting Polynomials

✎ *Add or subtract expressions.*

1) $(x^2 - 5) + (x^2 + 6) = $ _____

2) $(2x^2 - 6) - (3 - 2x^2) = $ _____

3) $(x^3 + 3x^2) - (x^3 + 6) = $ _____

4) $(4x^3 - x^2) + (6x^2 - 8x) = $ _____

5) $(2x^3 + 3x) - (5x^3 + 2) = $ _____

6) $(5x^3 - 2) + (2x^3 + 10) = $ _____

7) $(7x^3 + 5) - (9 - 4x^3) = $ _____

8) $(5x^2 + 3x^3) - (2x^3 + 6) = $ _____

9) $(8x^2 - x) + (4x - 8x^2) = $ _____

10) $(6x + 9x^2) - (5x + 2) = $ _____

11) $(7x^4 - 2x) - (6x - 2x^4) = $ _____

12) $(2x - 4x^3) - (9x^3 + 6x) = $ _____

13) $(8x^3 - 8x^2) - (6x^2 - 3x) = $ _____

14) $(9x^2 - 6) + (5x^2 - 4x^3) = $ _____

15) $(8x^3 + 3x^4) - (x^4 - 3x^3) = $ _____

16) $(-4x^3 - 2x) + (5x - 2x^3) = $ _____

17) $(9x - 5x^4) - (8x^4 + 4x) = $ _____

18) $(8x - 3x^2) - (7x^4 - 3x^2) = $ _____

19) $(9x^3 - 7) + (5x^3 - 4x^2) = $ _____

20) $(7x^3 + x^4) - (6x^4 - 5x^3) = $ _____

Chapter 10: Polynomials

Multiplying Monomials

✏️ **Simplify each expression.**

1) $4x^7 \times x^3 =$

2) $6y^2 \times 6y^3 =$

3) $-6z^7 \times 4z^4 =$

4) $5x^5y \times 8xy^3 =$

5) $-6xy^8 \times 3x^5y^3 =$

6) $7a^4b^2 \times 3a^8b =$

7) $5xy^5 \times 3x^3y^4 =$

8) $5p^5q^4 \times (-6pq^4) =$

9) $8s^6t^2 \times 6s^3t^7 =$

10) $(-8x^5y^2) \times 4x^6y^3 =$

11) $9xy^6z \times 3y^4z^2 =$

12) $12x^5y^4 \times 2x^8y =$

13) $4pq^5 \times (-7p^4q^8) =$

14) $9s^4t^2 \times (-5st^5) =$

15) $10p^3q^5 \times (-4p^4q^6) =$

16) $(-5p^2q^4r) \times 7pq^5r^3 =$

17) $(-9a^4b^7c^4) \times (-4a^7b) =$

18) $7u^5v^9 \times (-5u^{12}v^7) =$

19) $4u^4v^9z^2 \times (-5uv^8z) =$

20) $(-6xy^3z^5) \times 3x^3yz^7 =$

21) $6x^2y^3z^5 \times (-7x^4y^2z) =$

22) $7a^5b^8c^{12} \times 4a^6b^5c^9 =$

Chapter 10: Polynomials

Multiplying and Dividing Monomials

✎ **Simplify each expression.**

1) $(3x^5)(2x^2) =$

2) $(6x^5)(2x^4) =$

3) $(-7x^9)(2x^5) =$

4) $(7x^7y^9)(-5x^6y^6) =$

5) $(8x^5y^6)(3x^2y^5) =$

6) $(8yx^2)(7y^5x^3) =$

7) $(4x^2y)(2x^2y^3) =$

8) $(-2x^9y^4)(-9x^6y^8) =$

9) $(-5x^8y^2)(-6x^4y^5) =$

10) $(8x^8y)(-7x^4y^3) =$

11) $(9x^6y^2)(6x^7y^4) =$

12) $(8x^9y^5)(6x^5y^4) =$

13) $(-5x^8y^9)(7x^7y^8) =$

14) $(6x^2y^5)(5x^3y^2) =$

15) $(9x^5y^{12})(4x^7y^9) =$

16) $(-10x^{14}y^8)(2x^7y^5) =$

17) $\dfrac{6x^5y^7}{xy^6} =$

18) $\dfrac{9x^6y^6}{3x^4y} =$

19) $\dfrac{16x^4y^6}{4xy} =$

20) $\dfrac{-30x^9y^8}{5x^5y^4} =$

Chapter 10: Polynomials

Multiplying a Polynomial and a Monomial

✏ *Find each product.*

1) $x(x-5) =$

2) $2(3+x) =$

3) $x(x-7) =$

4) $x(x+9) =$

5) $2x(x-2) =$

6) $5(4x+3) =$

7) $4x(3x-4) =$

8) $x(5x+2y) =$

9) $3x(x-2y) =$

10) $6x(3x-4y) =$

11) $2x(3x-8) =$

12) $6x(4x-6y) =$

13) $3x(4x-2y) =$

14) $2x(2x-6y) =$

15) $5x(x^2+y^2) =$

16) $3x(2x^2-y^2) =$

17) $6(9x^2+3y^2) =$

18) $4x(-3x^2y+2y) =$

19) $-3(6x^2-5xy+3) =$

20) $6(x^2-4xy-3) =$

Chapter 10: Polynomials

Multiplying Binomials

✎ *Find each product.*

1) $(x-3)(x+4) =$ _____

2) $(x+3)(x+5) =$ _____

3) $(x-6)(x-7) =$ _____

4) $(x-9)(x-4) =$ _____

5) $(x-7)(x-5) =$ _____

6) $(x+6)(x+2) =$ _____

7) $(x-9)(x+3) =$ _____

8) $(x-8)(x-5) =$ _____

9) $(x+3)(x+7) =$ _____

10) $(x-9)(x+4) =$ _____

11) $(x+6)(x+6) =$ _____

12) $(x+7)(x+7) =$ _____

13) $(x-8)(x+7) =$ _____

14) $(x+9)(x+9) =$ _____

15) $(x-8)(x-8) =$ _____

16) $(x-9)(x+5) =$ _____

17) $(2x-5)(x+4) =$ _____

18) $(2x+6)(x+3) =$ _____

19) $(2x+4)(x+5) =$ _____

20) $(2x-3)(2x+2) =$ _____

Chapter 10: Polynomials

Factoring Trinomials

✏️ *Factor each trinomial.*

1) $x^2 + 5x + 4 =$

2) $x^2 + 5x + 6 =$

3) $x^2 - 4x + 3 =$

4) $x^2 - 10x + 25 =$

5) $x^2 - 13x + 40 =$

6) $x^2 + 8x + 12 =$

7) $x^2 - 6x - 27 =$

8) $x^2 - 14x + 48 =$

9) $x^2 + 15x + 56 =$

10) $x^2 - 5x - 36 =$

11) $x^2 + 12x + 36 =$

12) $x^2 + 16x + 63 =$

13) $x^2 + x - 72 =$

14) $x^2 + 18x + 81 =$

15) $x^2 - 16x + 64 =$

16) $x^2 - 18x + 81 =$

17) $2x^2 + 10x + 8 =$

18) $2x^2 + 4x - 6 =$

19) $2x^2 + 9x + 4 =$

20) $4x^2 + 4x - 24 =$

Chapter 10: Polynomials

Answers – Chapter 10

Simplifying Polynomials

1) $6x + 3$

2) $8x - 12$

3) $12x + 12$

4) $8x + 10$

5) $-24x + 21$

6) $6x^2 + 8x$

7) $-2x^3 + 6x^2$

8) $6x^3 - x^2 + 2x + 4$

9) $-9x^3 + 2x^2 + 5x$

10) $5x^4 - 2x^3 + 7x^2$

11) $6x^4 + 5x^3 - 3x^2$

12) $x^2 - 7x + 12$

13) $x^2 - x - 20$

14) $x^2 - 9x + 18$

15) $2x^2 + 21x + 40$

16) $3x^2 + 4x - 32$

17) $-10x^4 + 2x^3 - 8x^2 + 5x$

18) $-12x^3 - x^2 + 33$

19) $4x^3 + 3x^2 - 15x$

20) $-3x^3 - x^2 + 12$

21) $2x^5 - 2x^3 + 8x^2$

22) $3x^3 - 1$

Chapter 10: Polynomials

Adding and Subtracting Polynomials

1) $2x^2 + 1$
2) $4x^2 - 9$
3) $3x^2 - 6$
4) $4x^3 + 5x^2 - 8x$
5) $-3x^3 + 3x - 2$
6) $7x^3 + 8$
7) $11x^3 - 4$
8) $x^3 + 5x^2 - 6$
9) $3x$
10) $9x^2 + x - 2$
11) $9x^4 - 8x$
12) $-13x^3 - 4x$
13) $8x^3 - 14x^2 + 3x$
14) $-4x^3 + 14x^2 - 6$
15) $2x^4 + 11x^3$
16) $-6x^3 + 3x$
17) $-13x^4 + 5x$
18) $-7x^4 + 8x$
19) $14x^3 - 4x^2 - 7$
20) $-5x^4 + 12x^3$

Multiplying Monomials

1) $4x^{10}$
2) $36y^5$
3) $-24z^{11}$
4) $40x^6y^4$
5) $-18x^6y^{11}$
6) $21a^{12}b^3$
7) $15x^4y^9$
8) $-30p^6q^8$
9) $48s^9t^9$
10) $-32x^{11}y^5$
11) $27xy^{10}z^3$
12) $24x^{13}y^5$
13) $-28p^5q^{13}$
14) $-45s^5t^7$
15) $-40p^7q^{11}$
16) $-35p^3q^9r^4$
17) $36a^{11}b^8c^4$
18) $-35u^{17}v^{16}$
19) $-20u^5v^{17}z^3$
20) $-18x^4y^4z^{12}$
21) $-42x^6y^5z^6$
22) $28a^{11}b^{13}c^{21}$

Chapter 10: Polynomials

Multiplying and Dividing Monomials

1) $6x^7$
2) $12x^9$
3) $-14x^{14}$
4) $-35x^{13}y^{15}$
5) $24x^7y^{11}$
6) $56y^6x^5$
7) $8x^4y^4$
8) $18x^{15}y^{12}$
9) $30x^{12}y^7$
10) $-56x^{12}y^4$
11) $54x^{13}y^6$
12) $48x^{14}y^9$
13) $-35x^{15}y^{17}$
14) $30x^5y^7$
15) $36x^{12}y^{21}$
16) $-20x^{21}y^{13}$
17) $6x^4y$
18) $3x^2y^5$
19) $4x^3y^5$
20) $-6x^4y^4$

Multiplying a Polynomial and a Monomial

1) $x^2 - 5x$
2) $2x + 6$
3) $x^2 - 7x$
4) $x^2 + 9x$
5) $2x^2 - 4x$
6) $20x + 15$
7) $12x^2 - 16x$
8) $5x^2 + 2xy$
9) $3x^2 - 6xy$
10) $18x^2 - 24xy$
11) $6x^2 - 16x$
12) $24x^2 - 36xy$
13) $12x^2 - 6xy$
14) $4x^2 - 12xy$
15) $5x^3 + 5xy^2$
16) $6x^3 - 3xy^2$
17) $54x^2 + 18y^2$
18) $-12x^3y + 8xy$
19) $-18x^2 + 15xy - 9$
20) $6x^2 - 24xy - 18$

Chapter 10: Polynomials

Multiplying Binomials

1) $x^2 + x - 12$

2) $x^2 + 8x + 15$

3) $x^2 - 13x + 42$

4) $x^2 - 13x + 36$

5) $x^2 - 12x + 35$

6) $x^2 + 8x + 12$

7) $x^2 - 6x - 27$

8) $x^2 - 13x + 40$

9) $x^2 + 10x + 21$

10) $x^2 - 5x - 36$

11) $x^2 + 12x + 36$

12) $x^2 + 14x + 49$

13) $x^2 - x - 56$

14) $x^2 + 18x + 81$

15) $x^2 - 16x + 64$

16) $x^2 - 4x - 45$

17) $2x^2 + 3x - 20$

18) $2x^2 + 12x + 18$

19) $2x^2 + 14x + 20$

20) $4x^2 - 2x - 6$

Chapter 10: Polynomials

Factoring Trinomials

1) $(x+4)(x+1)$

2) $(x+3)(x+2)$

3) $(x-1)(x-3)$

4) $(x-5)(x-5)$

5) $(x-8)(x-5)$

6) $(x+6)(x+2)$

7) $(x-9)(x+3)$

8) $(x-8)(x-6)$

9) $(x+8)(x+7)$

10) $(x-9)(x+4)$

11) $(x+6)(x+6)$

12) $(x+7)(x+9)$

13) $(x-8)(x+9)$

14) $(x+9)(x+9)$

15) $(x-8)(x-8)$

16) $(x-9)(x-9)$

17) $2(x+1)(x+4)$

18) $2(x-1)(x+3)$

19) $(2x+1)(x+4)$

20) $(2x-4)(2x+6)$

Chapter 11: Geometry and Solid Figures

Math Topics that you'll learn in this Chapter:

- ✓ The Pythagorean Theorem
- ✓ Triangles
- ✓ Polygons
- ✓ Circles
- ✓ Trapezoids
- ✓ Cubes
- ✓ Rectangle Prisms
- ✓ Cylinder

Chapter 11: Geometry and Solid Figures

The Pythagorean Theorem

✎ *Do the following lengths form a right triangle?*

1) _____

2) _____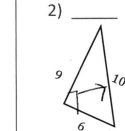

3) _____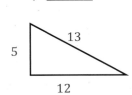

4) _____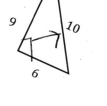

5) _____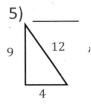

6) _____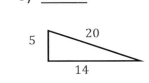

7) _____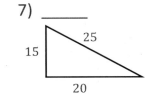

8) _____

✎ *Find the missing side.*

9) 25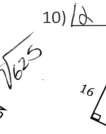

10) 12

11) 6

12) _____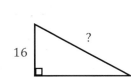

13) _____

14) _____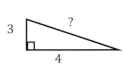

15) _____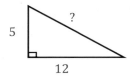

16) _____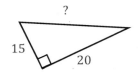

Chapter 11: Geometry and Solid Figures

Triangles

✎ **Find the measure of the unknown angle in each triangle.**

1) _____
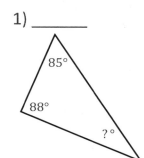

2) _____
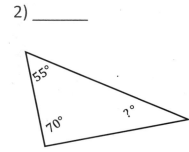

3) _____
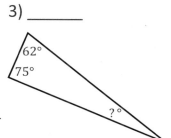

4) _____
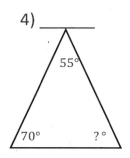

5) _____
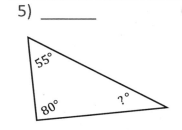

6) _____
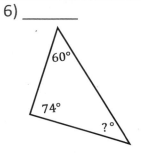

7) _____
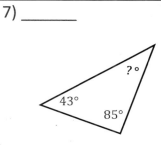

8) _____
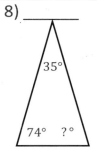

✎ **Find area of each triangle.**

9) _____
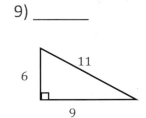

10) _____
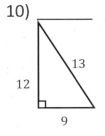

11) _____
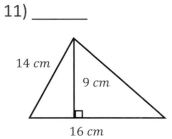

12) _____
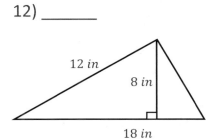

Chapter 11: Geometry and Solid Figures

Polygons

✎ *Find the perimeter of each shape.*

1) (square) _____ 2) _____ 3) _____ 4) (square) _____

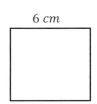 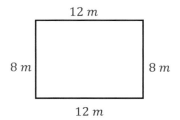 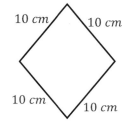 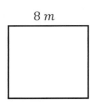

5) (regular hexagon) _____ 6) _____ 7) (parallelogram) _____ 8) (regular hexagon) _____

 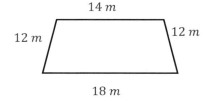 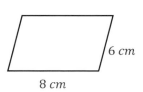 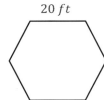

9) _____ 10) _____ 11) _____ 12) (regular hexagon) _____

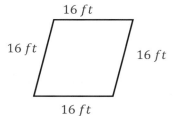  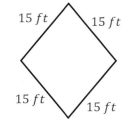 

108

www.EffortlessMath.com

Chapter 11: Geometry and Solid Figures

Circles

✎ **Find the Circumference of each circle.** ($\pi = 3.14$)

1) _____   2) _____   3) _____   4) _____   5) _____   6) _____

7) _____   8) _____   9) _____   10) _____   11) _____   12) _____

✎ **Complete the table below.** ($\pi = 3.14$)

	Radius	Diameter	Circumference	Area
Circle 1	2 inches	4 inches	12.56 inches	12.56 square inches
Circle 2		8 meters		
Circle 3				113.04 square feet
Circle 4			50.24 miles	
Circle 5		9 kilometers		
Circle 6	7 centimeters			
Circle 7		18 feet		
Circle 8				78.5 square meters
Circle 9			69.08 inches	
Circle 10	10 feet			

Chapter 11: Geometry and Solid Figures

Cubes

Length • Width • Height or c^3

✏️ **Find the volume of each cube.**

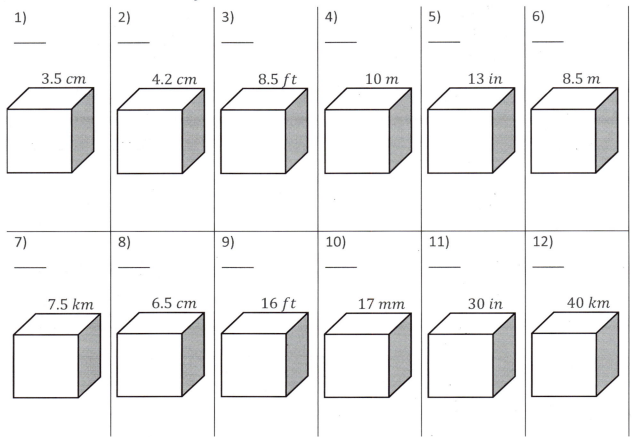

✏️ **Find the surface area of each cube.**

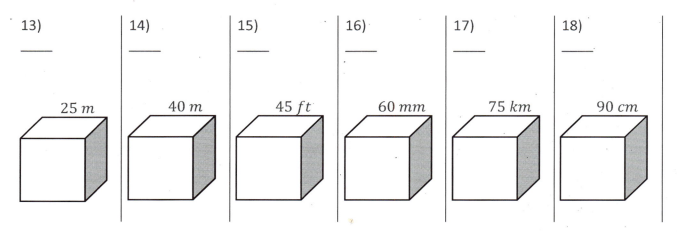

110

www.EffortlessMath.com

Chapter 11: Geometry and Solid Figures

Trapezoids

$A = \dfrac{a+b}{2} h$ or $A = \dfrac{b_1 + b_2}{2} h$

✏️ Find the area of each trapezoid.

1) _____   2) _____   3) _____   4) _____

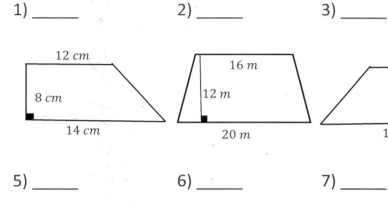
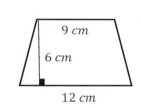

5) _____   6) _____   7) _____   8) _____

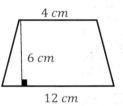
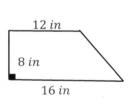
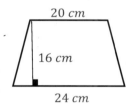
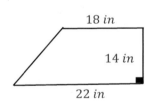

✏️ Solve.

9) A trapezoid has an area of 78 cm^2 and its height is 10 cm and one base is 8 cm. What is the other base length? _____

10) If a trapezoid has an area of 160 ft^2 and the lengths of the bases are 12 ft and 8 ft, find the height. _____

11) If a trapezoid has an area of 180 m^2 and its height is 8 m and one base is 10 m, find the other base length. _____

12) The area of a trapezoid is 150 ft^2 and its height is 20 ft. If one base of the trapezoid is 12 ft, what is the other base length? _____

$A = l \cdot w \cdot h$

Chapter 11: Geometry and Solid Figures

Rectangular Prisms

✎ Find the volume of each Rectangular Prism.

1) $240 m^3$ 2) ____   3) ____

4) ____   5) ____   6) ____

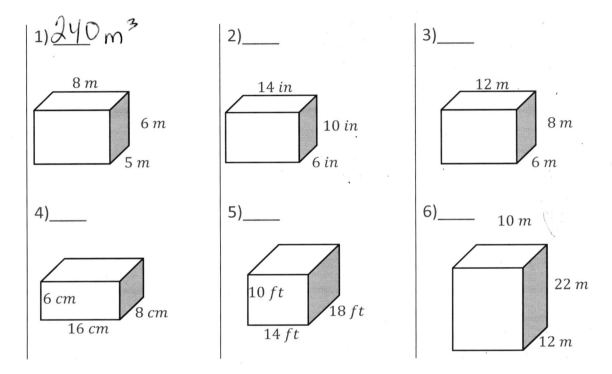

✎ Find the surface area of each Rectangular Prism. $2ab + 2bc + 2ac$

7) ____   8) ____   9) ____   10) ____

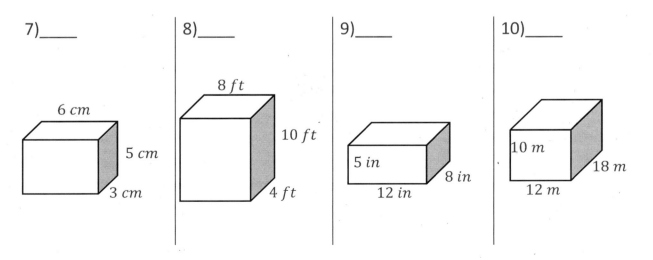

112

www.EffortlessMath.com

Chapter 11: Geometry and Solid Figures

Cylinder

$V = \pi r^2 h$

✏️ Find the volume of each Cylinder. ($\pi = 3.14$)

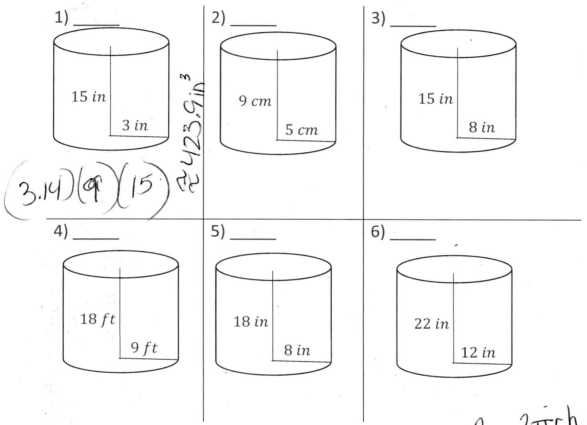

≈ 423.9 in³

(3.14)(9)(15)

✏️ Find the surface area of each Cylinder. ($\pi = 3.14$) $A = 2\pi r h + 2\pi r^2$

7) _____   8) _____   9) _____   10) _____

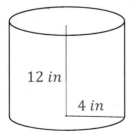 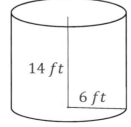 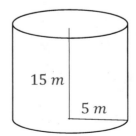

113

Chapter 11: Geometry and Solid Figures

Answers – Chapter 11

The Pythagorean Theorem

1) no
2) no
3) no
4) yes
5) no
6) no
7) yes
8) yes
9) 25
10) 12
11) 6
12) 34
13) 10
14) 5
15) 13
16) 25

Triangles

1) 7°
2) 55°
3) 43°
4) 55°
5) 45°
6) 46°
7) 52°
8) 71°
9) 27
10) 54
11) 72 cm^2
12) 72 in^2

Polygons

1) 24 cm
2) 40 m
3) 40 cm
4) 32 m
5) 96 m
6) 56 m
7) 28 cm
8) 120 ft
9) 64 ft
10) 80 in
11) 60 ft
12) 180 in

Chapter 11: Geometry and Solid Figures

Circles

1) $37.68\ in$
2) $62.8\ cm$
3) $119.32\ ft$
4) $75.36\ m$
5) $113.04\ cm$
6) $94.2\ miles$
7) $119.32\ in$
8) $138.16\ ft$
9) $157\ m$
10) $175.84\ m$
11) $219.8\ in$
12) $314\ ft$

	Radius	Diameter	Circumference	Area
Circle 1	2 inches	4 inches	12.56 inches	12.56 square inches
Circle 2	4 meters	8 meters	25.12 meters	50.24 square meters
Circle 3	6 feet	12 feet	37.68 feet	113.04 square feet
Circle 4	8 miles	16 miles	50.24 miles	200.96 square miles
Circle 5	4.5 kilometers	9 kilometers	28.26 kilometers	63.585 square kilometers
Circle 6	7 centimeters	14 centimeters	43.96 centimeters	153.86 square centimeters
Circle 7	9 feet	18 feet	56.52 feet	254.34 square feet
Circle 8	5 meters	10 meters	31.4 meters	78.5 square meters
Circle 9	11 inches	22 inches	69.08 inches	379.94 square inches
Circle 10	10 feet	20 feet	62.8 feet	314 square feet

Cubes

1) $42.875\ cm^3$
2) $74.088\ cm^3$
3) $614.125\ ft^3$
4) $1,000\ m^3$
5) $2,197\ in^3$
6) $614.125\ m^3$
7) $421.875\ km^3$
8) $274.625\ cm^3$
9) $4,096\ ft^3$
10) $4,913\ mm^3$
11) $27,000\ in^3$
12) $64,000\ km^3$
13) $3,750\ m^2$
14) $9,600\ m^2$
15) $12,150\ ft^2$
16) $21,600\ mm^2$
17) $33,750\ km^2$
18) $48,600\ cm^2$

Chapter 11: Geometry and Solid Figures

Trapezoids

1) $104\ cm^2$
2) $216\ m^2$
3) $54\ ft^2$
4) $63\ cm^2$
5) $48\ cm^2$
6) $112\ in^2$
7) $352\ cm^2$
8) $280\ in^2$
9) $7.6\ cm$
10) $16\ ft$
11) $35\ m$
12) $3\ ft$

Rectangular Prisms

1) $240\ m^3$
2) $840\ in^3$
3) $576\ m^3$
4) $768\ cm^3$
5) $2,520\ ft^3$
6) $2,640\ m^3$
7) $126\ cm^2$
8) $304\ ft^2$
9) $392\ in^2$
10) $1,032\ m^2$

Cylinder

1) $423.9\ in^3$
2) $706.5\ cm^3$
3) $3,014.4\ in^3$
4) $4,578.12\ ft^3$
5) $3,617.28\ in^3$
6) $9,947.52\ in^3$
7) $401.92\ in^2$
8) $439.6\ cm^2$
9) $753.6\ ft^2$
10) $628\ m^2$

www.EffortlessMath.com

Chapter 12: Statistics

Math Topics that you'll learn in this Chapter:

- ✓ Mean, Median, Mode, and Range of the Given Data
- ✓ Pie Graph
- ✓ Probability Problems
- ✓ Permutations and Combinations

Chapter 12: Statistics

Mean, Median, Mode, and Range of the Given Data

✎ **Find the values of the Given Data.**

1) 5, 12, 2, 2, 6

   Mode: _____   Range: _____

   Mean: _____   Median: _____

2) 5, 9, 3, 6, 4, 3

   Mode: _____   Range: _____

   Mean: _____   Median: _____

3) 12, 5, 8, 7, 8

   Mode: _____   Range: _____

   Mean: _____   Median: _____

4) 9, 7, 12, 7, 3, 4

   Mode: _____   Range: _____

   Mean: _____   Median: _____

5) 9, 7, 10, 5, 7, 4, 14

   Mode: _____   Range: _____

   Mean: _____   Median: _____

6) 8, 1, 6, 6, 9, 2, 17

   Mode: _____   Range: _____

   Mean: _____   Median: _____

7) 14, 5, 2, 7, 10, 7, 8, 13

   Mode: _____   Range: _____

   Mean: _____   Median: _____

8) 12, 14, 6, 4, 10, 8, 2

   Mode: _____   Range: _____

   Mean: _____   Median: _____

9) 17, 13, 16, 12, 14, 24

   Mode: _____   Range: _____

   Mean: _____   Median: _____

10) 18, 15, 10, 8, 4, 7, 8, 18

   Mode: _____   Range: _____

   Mean: _____   Median: _____

Chapter 12: Statistics

Pie Graph

🖎 **The circle graph below shows all Wilson's expenses for last month. Wilson spent $300 on his bills last month.**

Answer following questions based on the Pie graph.

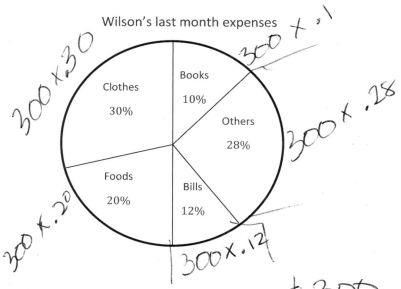

1) How much was Wilson's total expenses last month? $300

2) How much did Wilson spend on his clothes last month? 90

3) How much did Wilson spend for foods last month? 60

4) How much did Wilson spend on his books last month? 30

5) What fraction is Wilson's expenses for his bills and clothes out of his total expenses last month? $\frac{126}{300} = \frac{63}{150} = \frac{21}{50}$ 36 90

Chapter 12: Statistics

Probability Problems

1) If there are 15 red balls and 30 blue balls in a basket, what is the probability that Oliver will pick out a red ball from the basket? _____

Gender	Under 45	45 or older	Total
Male	12	6	18
Female	5	7	12
Total	17	13	30

2) The table above shows the distribution of age and gender for 30 employees in a company. If one employee is selected at random, what is the probability that the employee selected be either a female under age 45 or a male age 45 or older? _____

3) A number is chosen at random from 1 to 18. Find the probability of not selecting a composite number. (A composite number is a number that is divisible by itself, 1 and at least one other whole number) _____

4) There are 6 blue marbles, 8 red marbles, and 5 yellow marbles in a box. If Ava randomly selects a marble from the box, what is the probability of selecting a red or yellow marble? _____

5) A bag contains 20 balls: three green, six black, eight blue, a brown, a red and one white. If 19 balls are removed from the bag at random, what is the probability that a brown ball has been removed? _____

6) There are only red and blue marbles in a box. The probability of choosing a red marble in the box at random is one third. If there are 160 blue marbles, how many marbles are in the box? _____

Chapter 12: Statistics

Permutations and Combinations

✎ **Calculate the value of each.**

1) 5! = ____

2) 6! = ____

3) 8! = ____

4) 5! + 6! = ____

5) 8! + 3! = ____

6) 6! + 7! = ____

7) 8! + 4! = ____

8) 9! − 3! = ____

✎ **Solve each word problems.**

9) Sophia is baking cookies. She uses milk, flour and eggs. How many different orders of ingredients can she try? _____

10) William is planning for his vacation. He wants to go to restaurant, watch a movie, go to the beach, and play basketball. How many different ways of ordering are there for him? _____

11) How many 7 −digit numbers can be named using the digits 1, 2, 3, 4, 5, 6 and 7 without repetition? _____

12) In how many ways can 9 boys be arranged in a straight line? _____

13) In how many ways can 8 athletes be arranged in a straight line? _____

14) A professor is going to arrange her 6 students in a straight line. In how many ways can she do this? _____

15) How many code symbols can be formed with the letters for the word BLUE? _____

16) In how many ways a team of 8 basketball players can choose a captain and co-captain? _____

Chapter 12: Statistics

Answers – Chapter 12

Mean, Median, Mode, and Range of the Given Data

1) Mode: 2   Range: 10   Mean: 5.4   Median: 5

2) Mode: 3   Range: 6   Mean: 5   Median: 4.5

3) Mode: 8   Range: 7   Mean: 8   Median: 8

4) Mode: 7   Range: 9   Mean: 7   Median: 7

5) Mode: 7   Range: 10   Mean: 8   Median: 7

6) Mode: 6   Range: 16   Mean: 7   Median: 6

7) Mode: 7   Range: 12   Mean: 8.25   Median: 7.5

8) Mode: *no mode*   Range: 12   Mean: 8   Median: 8

9) Mode: *no mode*   Range: 12   Mean: 16   Median: 15

10) Mode: 8,18   Range: 14   Mean: 11   Median: 9

Pie Graph

1) $2,500

2) $750

3) $500

4) $250

5) $\frac{21}{50}$

Chapter 12: Statistics

Probability Problems

1) $\frac{1}{3}$

2) $\frac{11}{30}$

3) $\frac{7}{18}$

4) $\frac{13}{19}$

5) $\frac{19}{20}$

6) 240

Permutations and Combinations

1) 120

2) 720

3) 40,320

4) 840

5) 40,326

6) 5,760

7) 40,344

8) 362,874

9) 6

10) 24

11) 5,040

12) 362,880

13) 40,320

14) 720

15) 24

16) 56

Chapter 13: Functions Operations

Math Topics that you'll learn in this Chapter:

- ✓ Function Notation and Evaluation
- ✓ Adding and Subtracting Functions
- ✓ Multiplying and Dividing Functions
- ✓ Composition of Functions

Chapter 13: Functions Operations

Function Notation and Evaluation

✎ **Evaluate each function.**

1) $f(x) = x - 3$, find $f(-2)$

2) $g(x) = x + 5$, find $g(6)$

3) $h(x) = x + 8$, find $h(2)$

4) $f(x) = -x - 7$, find $f(5)$

5) $f(x) = 2x - 7$, find $f(-1)$

6) $w(x) = -2 - 4x$, find $w(5)$

7) $g(n) = 6n - 3$, find $g(-2)$

8) $h(x) = -8x + 12$, find $h(3)$

9) $k(n) = 14 - 3n$, find $k(3)$

10) $g(x) = 4x - 4$, find $g(-2)$

11) $k(n) = 8n - 7$, find $k(4)$

12) $w(n) = -2n + 14$, find $w(5)$

13) $h(x) = 5x - 18$, find $h(8)$

14) $g(n) = 2n^2 + 2$, find $g(5)$

15) $f(x) = 3x^2 - 13$, find $f(2)$

16) $g(n) = 5n^2 + 7$, find $g(-3)$

17) $h(n) = 5n^2 - 10$, find $h(4)$

18) $g(x) = -3x^2 - 6x$, find $g(2)$

19) $k(n) = 4n^3 + n$, find $k(-5)$

20) $f(x) = -3x + 10$, find $f(3x)$

21) $k(a) = 4a + 9$, find $k(a - 1)$

22) $h(x) = 8x + 4$, find $h(5x)$

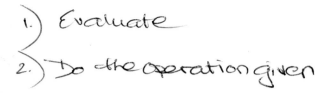
1.) Evaluate
2.) Do the operation given

Chapter 13: Functions Operations

Adding and Subtracting Functions

✎ **Perform the indicated operation.**

1) $f(x) = x + 4$
   $g(x) = 2x + 5$
   Find $(f - g)(2)$
   ___

2) $g(x) = x - 2$
   $f(x) = -x - 6$
   Find $(g - f)(-2)$
   ___

3) $h(t) = 4t + 4$
   $g(t) = 3t + 2$
   Find $(h + g)(-1)$
   ___

4) $g(a) = 5a - 7$
   $f(a) = a^2 + 3$
   Find $(g + f)(2)$
   ___

5) $g(x) = 4x - 5$
   $f(x) = 6x^2 + 5$
   Find $(g - f)(-2)$
   ___

6) $h(x) = x^2 + 3$
   $g(x) = -4x + 1$
   Find $(h + g)(4)$
   ___

7) $f(x) = -3x - 9$
   $g(x) = x^2 + 5$
   Find $(f - g)(6)$
   ___

8) $h(n) = -4n^2 + 9$
   $g(n) = 5n + 6$
   Find $(h - g)(5)$
   ___

9) $g(x) = 4x^2 - 3x - 1$
   $f(x) = 6x + 10$
   Find $(g - f)(a)$
   ___

10) $g(t) = -6t - 7$
    $f(t) = -t^2 + 3t + 15$
    Find $(g + f)(t)$
    ___

www.EffortlessMath.com

Chapter 13: Functions Operations

Multiplying and Dividing Functions

✎ **Perform the indicated operation.**

1) $g(x) = x + 6$
   $f(x) = x + 4$
   Find $(g.f)(2)$

2) $f(x) = 3x$
   $h(x) = -x + 5$
   Find $(f.h)(-2)$

3) $g(a) = a + 5$
   $h(a) = 2a - 4$
   Find $(g.h)(4)$

4) $f(x) = 3x + 2$
   $h(x) = 2x - 3$
   Find $(\frac{f}{h})(2)$

5) $f(x) = a^2 - 2$
   $g(x) = -4 + 3a$
   Find $(\frac{f}{g})(2)$

6) $g(a) = 4a + 6$
   $f(a) = 2a - 8$
   Find $(\frac{g}{f})(3)$

7) $g(t) = t^2 + 6$
   $h(t) = 2t - 3$
   Find $(g.h)(-3)$

8) $g(x) = x^2 + 3x + 4$
   $h(x) = 2x + 6$
   Find $(g.h)(2)$

9) $g(a) = 2a^2 - 5a + 1$
   $f(a) = 2a^3 - 6$
   Find $(\frac{g}{f})(4)$

10) $g(x) = -3x^2 + 4 - 2x$
    $f(x) = x^2 - 5$
    Find $(g.f)(3)$

Step 1) plug the innermost term into the g or f (or whatever variable given
Step 2) put that answer into the outside parenthesis

Chapter 13: Functions Operations ★ work inside out

Composition of Functions

✏️ Using $f(x) = x + 6$ and $g(x) = 3x$, find:

1) $f(g(1)) = $ _____

2) $f(g(-1)) = $ _____

3) $g(f(-3)) = $ _____

4) $g(f(4)) = $ _____

5) $f(g(2)) = $ _____

6) $g(f(3)) = $ _____

✏️ Using $f(x) = 2x + 5$ and $g(x) = x - 2$, find:

7) $g(f(2)) = $ _____

8) $g(f(-2)) = $ _____

9) $f(g(5)) = $ _____

10) $f(f(4)) = $ _____

11) $g(f(3)) = $ _____

12) $g(f(-3)) = $ _____

✏️ Using $f(x) = 4x - 2$ and $g(x) = x - 5$, find:

13) $g(f(-2)) = $ _____

14) $f(f(4)) = $ _____

15) $f(g(5)) = $ _____

16) $f(f(3)) = $ _____

17) $g(f(-3)) = $ _____

18) $g(g(6)) = $ _____

✏️ Using $f(x) = 6x + 2$ and $g(x) = 2x - 3$, find:

19) $f(g(-3)) = $ _____

20) $g(f(5)) = $ _____

21) $f(g(4)) = $ _____

22) $f(f(3)) = $ _____

Chapter 13: Functions Operations

Answers – Chapter 13

Function Notation and Evaluation

1) -5
2) 11
3) 10
4) -12
5) -9
6) -22
7) -15
8) -12
9) 5
10) -12
11) 25
12) 4
13) 22
14) 52
15) -1
16) 52
17) 70
18) -24
19) -505
20) $-9x + 10$
21) $4a + 5$
22) $40x + 4$

Adding and Subtracting Functions

1) -3
2) 0
3) -1
4) 10
5) -42
6) 4
7) -68
8) -122
9) $4a^2 - 9a - 11$
10) $-t^2 - 3t + 8$

Multiplying and Dividing Functions

1) 48
2) -42
3) 36
4) 8
5) 1
6) -9
7) -135
8) 140
9) $\dfrac{13}{122}$
10) -116

Chapter 13: Functions Operations

Composition of Functions

1) $f(g(1)) = 9$
2) $f(g(-1)) = 3$
3) $g(f(-3)) = 9$
4) $g(f(4)) = 30$
5) $f(g(2)) = 12$
6) $g(f(3)) = 27$
7) $g(f(2)) = 7$
8) $g(f(-2)) = -1$

9) $f(g(5)) = 11$
10) $f(f(4)) = 31$
11) $g(f(3)) = 9$
12) $g(f(-3)) = -3$
13) $g(f(-2)) = -15$
14) $f(f(4)) = 54$
15) $f(g(5)) = -2$
16) $f(f(3)) = 38$

17) $g(f(-3)) = -19$
18) $g(g(6)) = -4$
19) $f(g(-3)) = -52$
20) $g(f(5)) = 61$
21) $f(g(4)) = 32$
22) $f(f(3)) = 122$

Time to Test

Time to refine your skill with a practice examination

In this section, there are two complete PERT Mathematics Tests. Take these tests to simulate the test day experience. After you've finished, score your test using the answer key.

Before You Start

- You'll need a pencil, a timer, and a four-function calculator to take the test.
- Use the answer sheet provided to record your answers. (You can cut it out or photocopy it)
- For each question there are four possible answers. Choose which one is best.
- After you've finished the test, review the answer key to see where you went wrong and what areas you need to improve.

Good Luck!

PERT Mathematics

Practice Test 1

30 questions

Total time for this section: No time limit

You may use a calculator on this Test.

PERT Mathematics Practice Test Answer Sheet

Remove (or photocopy) this answer sheet and use it to complete the practice test.

PERT Mathematics Practice Test 1 Answer Sheet					
1	Ⓐ Ⓑ Ⓒ Ⓓ	13	Ⓐ Ⓑ Ⓒ Ⓓ	25	Ⓐ Ⓑ Ⓒ Ⓓ
2	Ⓐ Ⓑ Ⓒ Ⓓ	14	Ⓐ Ⓑ Ⓒ Ⓓ	26	Ⓐ Ⓑ Ⓒ Ⓓ
3	Ⓐ Ⓑ Ⓒ Ⓓ	15	Ⓐ Ⓑ Ⓒ Ⓓ	27	Ⓐ Ⓑ Ⓒ Ⓓ
4	Ⓐ Ⓑ Ⓒ Ⓓ	16	Ⓐ Ⓑ Ⓒ Ⓓ	28	Ⓐ Ⓑ Ⓒ Ⓓ
5	Ⓐ Ⓑ Ⓒ Ⓓ	17	Ⓐ Ⓑ Ⓒ Ⓓ	29	Ⓐ Ⓑ Ⓒ Ⓓ
6	Ⓐ Ⓑ Ⓒ Ⓓ	18	Ⓐ Ⓑ Ⓒ Ⓓ	30	Ⓐ Ⓑ Ⓒ Ⓓ
7	Ⓐ Ⓑ Ⓒ Ⓓ	19	Ⓐ Ⓑ Ⓒ Ⓓ		
8	Ⓐ Ⓑ Ⓒ Ⓓ	20	Ⓐ Ⓑ Ⓒ Ⓓ		
9	Ⓐ Ⓑ Ⓒ Ⓓ	21	Ⓐ Ⓑ Ⓒ Ⓓ		
10	Ⓐ Ⓑ Ⓒ Ⓓ	22	Ⓐ Ⓑ Ⓒ Ⓓ		
11	Ⓐ Ⓑ Ⓒ Ⓓ	23	Ⓐ Ⓑ Ⓒ Ⓓ		
12	Ⓐ Ⓑ Ⓒ Ⓓ	24	Ⓐ Ⓑ Ⓒ Ⓓ		

PERT Math Practice Workbook

1) Simplify $5x^2y^3(2x^2y)^3 = ?$

   A. $10x^4y^6$

   B. $40x^8y^6$

   C. $20x^7y^5$

   D. $40x^3y^8$

2) If x is directly proportional to the square of y, and $y = 2$ when $x = 12$, then when $x = 75$ $y = ?$

   A. $\frac{1}{5}$

   B. 1

   C. 5

   D. 12

3) Jack earns $616 for his first 44 hours of work in a week and is then paid 1.5 times his regular hourly rate for any additional hours. This week, Jack needs $826 to pay his rent, bills and other expenses. How many hours must he work to make enough money in this week?

   A. 40

   B. 43

   C. 48

   D. 54

4) Jack types 72 words per minute. How many words does he type in 15 seconds?

   A. 18

   B. 20

   C. 22

   D. 24

PERT Mathematics Practice Test 1

5) Which of the following is the same as: 0.000,000,000,000,042,121?

   A. 4.2121×10^{14}

   B. 4.2121×10^{-14}

   C. $42,121 \times 10^{-10}$

   D. 42.121×10^{-13}

6) A shirt costing $200 is discounted 15%. After a month, the shirt is discounted another 15%. Which of the following expressions can be used to find the selling price of the shirt?

   A. $(200)(0.70)$

   B. $(200) - 200(0.30)$

   C. $(200)(0.15) - (200)(0.15)$

   D. $(200)(0.85)(0.85)$

7) Which of the following points lies on the line with equation $2x + 4y = 10$?

   A. $(2, 1)$

   B. $(-1, 3)$

   C. $(-2, 2)$

   D. $(2, 2)$

8) A student gets 85% of a test with 40 questions. How many answers did the student solve correctly?

   A. 25

   B. 28

   C. 34

   D. 36

9) A ladder leans against a wall forming a 60° angle between the ground and the ladder. If the bottom of the ladder is 30 feet away from the wall, how long is the ladder?

A. 30 feet

B. 40 feet

C. 50 feet

D. 60 feet

10) To buy a new computer, Emma borrowed $2,500 at 8% interest for 6 years. How much interest did she pay?

A. $150

B. $1,200

C. $1,500

D. $2,400

11) What is the value of y in the following system of equation?

$$3x - 4y = -40$$
$$-x + 2y = 10$$

A. $y = 5$

B. $y = 2$

C. $y = -2$

D. $y = -5$

12) From last year, the price of gasoline has increased from $1.25 per gallon to $1.75 per gallon. The new price is what percent of the original price?

A. 72%

B. 120%

C. 140%

D. 160%

13) If $b = 2$ and $\frac{a}{4} = b$, what is the value of $a^2 + 4b$?

   A. 66

   B. 72

   C. 76

   D. 81

14) The average of $13, 15, 20$ and x is 15. What is the value of x?

   A. 10

   B. 12

   C. 14

   D. 18

15) If n is an even integer that is less than -3.34, what is the greatest possible value of n?

   A. -1

   B. -2

   C. -4

   D. -5

16) $3^4 + 4^4 = ?$

   A. 240

   B. 337

   C. 421

   D. 330

17) Integer x is evenly divisible by 4. Which expression below is also evenly divisible by 4?

   A. $x + 1$

   B. $2x + 1$

   C. $2x + 4$

   D. $3x + 2$

18) Sara has a box containing 5 blue balls, 8 red balls, and 3 green balls. If she removes one ball at random, what is the probability that it will not be blue?

A. $\frac{5}{16}$

B. $\frac{11}{16}$

C. $\frac{10}{11}$

D. $\frac{5}{11}$

19) On the number line below, point M is located on line segment ON so that $OM = \frac{1}{3}MN$. What is the position of point M?

A. -4.2

B. -3.5

C. -1.5

D. 1.5

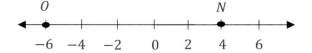

20) Jack rides 160 kilometers in 1 hour 20 minutes. At that rate, how many meters does he ride per minute?

A. 1,000 meters

B. 1,500 meters

C. 2,000 meters

D. 2,500 meters

21) The sum of two consecutive integer is -13. If 2 is added to the smaller integer and 3 is subtract from the larger integer, what is the product of the two resulting integers?

A. 5

B. 18

C. 28

D. 45

PERT Mathematics Practice Test 1

22) The capacity of a red box is 20% bigger than the capacity of a blue box. If the red box can hold 30 equal sized books, how many of the same books can the blue box hold?

   A. 9
   B. 15
   C. 21
   D. 25

23) Which of the following is equal to the expression below?

$$(2x + y)(x - 2y)$$

   A. $4x^2 - 2y^2$
   B. $2x^2 - 2y^2$
   C. $2x^2 - 2y^2 - 2xy$
   D. $2x^2 - 2y^2 - 3xy$

24) What is the slope of a line that is perpendicular to the line $4x - 2y = 12$?

   A. -2
   B. $-\frac{1}{2}$
   C. 4
   D. 12

25) Kim spent $35 for pants. This was $10 less than triple what she spent for a shirt. How much was the shirt?

   A. $11
   B. $13
   C. $15
   D. $17

26) What is the greatest integer less than $-\frac{32}{5}$?

   A. 0
   B. -2
   C. -4
   D. -7

27) The measure of the angles of a triangle are in the ratio $1:3:5$. What is the measure of the largest angle?

   A. $20°$
   B. $45°$
   C. $85°$
   D. $100°$

28) In the figure below, line A is parallel to line B. what is the value of x?

   A. 28
   B. 46
   C. 50
   D. 65

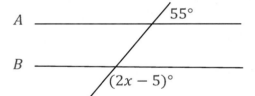

29) Simplify: $\dfrac{\left(\frac{40(x+1)}{4}\right)-10}{12}$?

   A. $\frac{12}{5}x$
   B. $\frac{5}{6}x$
   C. $\frac{3}{7}x$
   D. $\frac{5}{12}x$

30) The area of a circle is $144\pi \ ft^2$. Which of the following can be the diameter of the circle?

A. $12 \ ft$

B. $28 \ ft$

C. $24 \ ft$

D. $32 \ ft$

PERT Mathematics

Practice Test 2

30 questions

Total time for this section: No time limit

You may use a calculator on this Test.

PERT Mathematics Practice Test Answer Sheet

Remove (or photocopy) this answer sheet and use it to complete the practice test.

PERT Mathematics Practice Test 2 Answer Sheet

1	Ⓐ Ⓑ Ⓒ Ⓓ	13	Ⓐ Ⓑ Ⓒ Ⓓ	25	Ⓐ Ⓑ Ⓒ Ⓓ
2	Ⓐ Ⓑ Ⓒ Ⓓ	14	Ⓐ Ⓑ Ⓒ Ⓓ	26	Ⓐ Ⓑ Ⓒ Ⓓ
3	Ⓐ Ⓑ Ⓒ Ⓓ	15	Ⓐ Ⓑ Ⓒ Ⓓ	27	Ⓐ Ⓑ Ⓒ Ⓓ
4	Ⓐ Ⓑ Ⓒ Ⓓ	16	Ⓐ Ⓑ Ⓒ Ⓓ	28	Ⓐ Ⓑ Ⓒ Ⓓ
5	Ⓐ Ⓑ Ⓒ Ⓓ	17	Ⓐ Ⓑ Ⓒ Ⓓ	29	Ⓐ Ⓑ Ⓒ Ⓓ
6	Ⓐ Ⓑ Ⓒ Ⓓ	18	Ⓐ Ⓑ Ⓒ Ⓓ	30	Ⓐ Ⓑ Ⓒ Ⓓ
7	Ⓐ Ⓑ Ⓒ Ⓓ	19	Ⓐ Ⓑ Ⓒ Ⓓ		
8	Ⓐ Ⓑ Ⓒ Ⓓ	20	Ⓐ Ⓑ Ⓒ Ⓓ		
9	Ⓐ Ⓑ Ⓒ Ⓓ	21	Ⓐ Ⓑ Ⓒ Ⓓ		
10	Ⓐ Ⓑ Ⓒ Ⓓ	22	Ⓐ Ⓑ Ⓒ Ⓓ		
11	Ⓐ Ⓑ Ⓒ Ⓓ	23	Ⓐ Ⓑ Ⓒ Ⓓ		
12	Ⓐ Ⓑ Ⓒ Ⓓ	24	Ⓐ Ⓑ Ⓒ Ⓓ		

PERT Math Practice Workbook

1) In the xy-plane, the point $(1, 2)$ and $(-1, 6)$ are on line A. Which of the following points could also be on line A?

   A. $(-3, 2)$

   B. $(-3, 5)$

   C. $(-2, 5)$

   D. $(3, -2)$

2) Four one – foot rulers can be split among how many users to leave each with $\frac{1}{3}$ of a ruler?

   A. 4

   B. 6

   C. 12

   D. 24

3) The set of possible values of n is $\{5, 3, 7\}$. What is the set of possible values of m if $2m = n + 5$?

   A. $\{2, 4, 7\}$

   B. $\{5, 4, 6\}$

   C. $\{3, 2, 5\}$

   D. $\{4, 5, 8\}$

4) Solve for x: $7x + 3 - 2(2x + 1) = 13$

   A. $x = 4$

   B. $x = 6$

   C. $x = -2$

   D. $x = -5$

5) If $x = 25$, then which of the following equations are correct?

   A. $x + 10 = 40$

   B. $4x = 100$

   C. $3x = 70$

   D. $\frac{x}{2} = 12$

6) Jack scored a mean of 80 per test in his first 4 tests. In his 5th test, he scored 90. What was Jack's mean score for the 5 tests?

   A. 70

   B. 75

   C. 80

   D. 82

7) The volume of a cube is less than $64\ m^3$. Which of the following can be the cube's side?

   A. $2\ m$

   B. $4\ m$

   C. $8\ m$

   D. $11\ m$

8) Simplify the expression. $(5x^3 - 8x^2 + 2x^4) - (4x^2 - 2x^4 + 2x^3)$

   A. $8x^4 + 7x^3 - 8x^2$

   B. $5x^4 + x^3 - 9x^2$

   C. $4x^4 + 3x^3 - 12x^2$

   D. $5x^4 + 2x^3 - 8x^2$

9) If $a = 120°$ and $b = 98°$, what is the value of the c?(Figure not drawn to scale.)

   A. 19°

   B. 22°

   C. 35°

   D. 45°

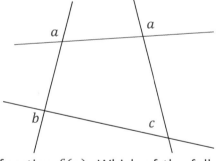

10) The following table represents the value of x and function $f(x)$. Which of the following could be the equation of the function $f(x)$?

   A. $f(x) = x^2 - 5$

   B. $f(x) = x^2 - 1$

   C. $f(x) = \sqrt{x+2}$

   D. $f(x) = \sqrt{x} + 4$

x	$f(x)$
1	5
4	6
9	7
16	8

11) What is the area of an isosceles right triangle that has one leg that measures 6 cm?

   A. 6 cm^2

   B. 12 cm^2

   C. 18 cm^2

   D. 36 cm^2

12) If $0.00104 = \frac{104}{x}$, what is the value of x?

   A. 1,000

   B. 10,000

   C. 100,000

   D. 1,000,000

13) A bag is filled with numbered cards from 1 to 15 and picked on at random. What is the probability that the card picked is number 8?

   A. $\frac{8}{15}$

   B. $\frac{7}{15}$

   C. $\frac{2}{15}$

   D. $\frac{1}{15}$

14) What is the value of x in the figure below?

   A. $32°$

   B. $46°$

   C. $54°$

   D. $63°$

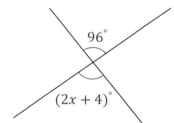

15) What is the value of the following expression? $|-5| + 9 \times 2\frac{1}{3} + (-3)^2 =$

   A. 26

   B. 35

   C. 43

   D. 51

16) How many different two-digit numbers can be formed from the digits 6, 7, and 5, if the numbers must be even and no digit can be repeated?

   A. 1

   B. 2

   C. 3

   D. 4

17) A rectangular concrete driveway is 25 feet long, 6 feet wide, and 24 inches thick. What is the volume of the concrete?

   A. $300\ ft^3$

   B. $660\ ft^3$

   C. $963\ ft^3$

   D. $1,800\ ft^3$

18) If $\frac{2y}{x} - \frac{y}{3x} = \frac{(\ldots)}{3x}$ and $x \neq 0$, what expression is represented by $(\ldots)$?

   A. $2y + 4$

   B. $3y - 6$

   C. $5y$

   D. $6y$

19) If $360\ kg$ of vegetables is packed in 90 boxes, how much vegetables will each box contain?

   A. $2.5\ kg$

   B. $3\ kg$

   C. $4\ kg$

   D. $6.5\ kg$

20) Each number in a sequence is 4 more than twice the number that comes just before it. If 84 is a number in the sequence, what number comes just before it?

   A. 26

   B. 35

   C. 40

   D. 52

21) 38 is What percent of 50?

   A. 45%

   B. 52%

   C. 64%

   D. 76%

22) A rectangle has 14 cm wide and 5 cm length. What is the perimeter of this rectangle?

   A. 38 cm

   B. 43 cm

   C. 49 cm

   D. 58 cm

23) What is the product of all possible values of x in the following equation?

$$|x - 10| = 3$$

   A. 7

   B. 13

   C. 80

   D. 91

24) What is the value of the following expression? $3\frac{1}{4} + 2\frac{4}{16} + 1\frac{3}{8} + 5\frac{1}{2}$

   A. $3\frac{10}{14}$

   B. $4\frac{1}{2}$

   C. $12\frac{4}{16}$

   D. $12\frac{3}{8}$

25) A certain insect has a mass of 85 milligrams. What is the insect's mass in grams?

   A. 0.08

   B. 0.085

   C. 0.85

   D. 85

26) If $m = 6$ and $n = -3$, what is the value of $\frac{5-9(3+n)}{3m-5(2-n)} = ?$

   A. $-\frac{4}{7}$

   B. $-\frac{5}{7}$

   C. $\frac{3}{7}$

   D. $\frac{2}{7}$

27) Clara has 28 cookies. She is inviting 7 friends to a party. How many cookies will each friends get?

   A. 2

   B. 4

   C. 7

   D. 8

28) How long will it take to receive $360 in investment of $240 at the rate of 10% simple interest?

   A. 9 years

   B. 15 years

   C. 18 years

   D. 21 years

29) How many hours are there in 1,800 minutes?

   A. 20 hours

   B. 25 hours

   C. 30 hours

   D. 33 hours

30) A shoes originally priced at $45.00 was on sale for 15% off. Nick received a 20% employee discount applied to the sale price. How much did Nick pay for the shoes?

A. $30.60

B. $34.50

C. $37.30

D. $42.25

IF YOU FINISH BEFORE TIME IS CALLED, YOU MAY CHECK YOUR WORK ON THIS TEST.

STOP

PERT Math Practice Tests Answer Keys

Now, it's time to review your results to see where you went wrong and what areas you need to improve.

PERT Math Practice Test 1				PERT Math Practice Test 2			
1	B	21	D	1	D	21	D
2	C	22	D	2	C	22	A
3	D	23	D	3	B	23	D
4	A	24	B	D	A	24	D
5	B	25	C	5	B	25	B
6	D	26	D	6	D	26	B
7	B	27	D	7	A	27	B
8	C	28	D	8	C	28	B
9	D	29	B	9	B	29	C
10	B	30	C	10	D	30	A
11	D			11	11	C	
12	C			12	12	C	
13	B			13	13	D	
14	B			14	14	B	
15	C			15	15	B	
16	B			16	16	B	
17	C			17	17	A	
18	B			18	18	C	
19	B			19	19	C	
20	C			20	20	C	

PERT Mathematics Practice Tests Answers and Explanations

PERT Mathematics Practice Test 1
Answers and Explanations

1) Choice B is correct

Simplify. $5x^2y^3(2x^2y)^3 = 5x^2y^3(8x^6y^3) = 40x^8y^6$

2) Choice C is correct

x is directly proportional to the square of y. Then $x = cy^2 \rightarrow 12 = c(2)^2 \rightarrow 12 = 4c \rightarrow$:

$c = \frac{12}{4} = 3$. The relationship between x and y is: $x = 3y^2, x = 75$

$75 = 3y^2 \rightarrow y^2 = \frac{75}{3} = 25 \rightarrow y = 5$

3) Choice D is correct

The amount of money that Jack earns for one hour: $\frac{\$616}{44} = \$14$

A number of additional hours that he works to make enough money is: $\frac{\$826 - \$616}{1.5 \times \$14} = 10$

Number of total hours is: $44 + 10 = 54$

4) Choice A is correct

15 second is one fourth of a minute. One fourth of 72 is 18. $72 \div 4 = 18$. Jack types 18 words in 15 seconds.

5) Choice B is correct

In scientific notation all numbers are written in the form of: $m \times 10^n$, where m is between 1 and 10. To find an equivalent value of 0.000,000,000,000,042,121, move the decimal point to the right so that you have a number that is between 1 and 10. Then: 4.2121. Now, determine how many places the decimal moved in step 1, then put it as the power of 10. We moved the decimal point 14 places. Then: 10^{-14} when the decimal moved to the right, the exponent is negative. Then: $0.000,000,000,000,042,121 = 4.2121 \times 10^{-14}$.

6) Choice D is correct

To find the discount, multiply the number by $(100\% - rate\ of\ discount)$.

Therefore, for the first discount we get: $(200)(100\% - 15\%) = (200)(0.85) = 170$

For the next 15% discount: $(200)(0.85)(0.85)$

7) Choice B is correct

Plug in each pair of numbers in the equation:

A. $(2, 1)$: $2(2) + 4(1) = 8$

B. $(-1, 3)$: $2(-1) + 4(3) = 10$

C. $(-2, 2)$: $2(-2) + 4(2) = 4$

D. $(2, 2)$: $2(2) + 4(2) = 12$

Only choice B is equal to 10.

8) Choice C is correct

85% of 40 is: $0.85 \times 40 = 34$. So, the student solves 34 questions correctly.

9) Choice D is correct

The relationship among all sides of special right triangle

$30° - 60° - 90°$ is provided in this triangle:

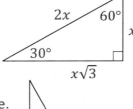

In this triangle, the opposite side of $30°$ angle is half of the hypotenuse.

Draw the shape for this question:

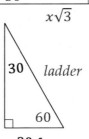

The ladder is the hypotenuse. Therefore, the ladder is $60\ feet$.

10) Choice B is correct

Use simple interest formula: $I = prt$ ($I = interest, p = principal, r = rate, t = time$)

Simple interest $I = 2,500 \times 0.08 \times 6 = 1,200$

She will pay $1,200 interest at the end of 6 years.

11) Choice D is correct

Solve the system of equations by elimination method:

$3x - 4y = -40$
$-x + 2y = 10$ Multiply the second equation by 3, then add it to the first equation.

$\begin{array}{l} 3x - 4y = -40 \\ 3(-x + 2y = 10) \end{array} \Rightarrow \begin{array}{l} 3x - 4y = -40 \\ -3x + 6y = 30) \end{array} \Rightarrow$ add the equations $2y = -10 \Rightarrow y = -5$

PERT Mathematics Practice Tests Answers and Explanations

12) Choice C is correct

The question is this: 1.75 is what percent of 1.25? $\frac{1.75}{1.25} = 1.40 = 140\%$

13) Choice B is correct

First, use the given information to calculate the value of a: $\frac{a}{4} = b \rightarrow \frac{a}{4} = 2 \rightarrow a = 8$

Now, calculate $a^2 + 4b$ by substituting $a = 8$ and $b = 2 \rightarrow (8)^2 + 4(2) = 72$

14) Choice B is correct

Use the average formula: $average = \frac{sum\ of\ terms}{number\ of\ terms} \Rightarrow 15 = \frac{13+15+20+x}{4} \Rightarrow 60 = 48 + x \Rightarrow x = 60 - 48 = 12$

15) Choice C is correct

The two greatest integers less than -3.34 are -4 and -5. Since -5 is odd, the answer is -4.

16) Choice B is correct

Adding exponents is done by calculating each exponent first and then adding:

$3^4 + 4^4 = 81 + 256 = 337$

17) Choice C is correct

Since integer x is evenly divisible by 4, substitute 4 for x in the answer choices to determine which expression is also divisible by 4: Let $x = 4$.

Choice A: $x + 1 = 4 + 1 = 5$ this is NOT divisible by 4.

Choice B: $2x + 1 = 2(4) + 1 = 9$ this is NOT divisible by 4.

Choice C: $2x + 4 = 2(4) + 4 = 12$ this is divisible by 4.

Choice D: $3x + 2 = 3(4) + 1 = 13$ this is NOT divisible by 4.

So, choice C is correct.

18) Choice B is correct

There are currently 16 balls in the bag $(5 + 8 + 3)$. Of those balls, 11 are not blue. So, the probability of choosing a ball that is not blue is $\frac{11}{16}$.

19) Choice B is correct

$ON = 4 - (-6) = 10$ units. Let $x = OM$. Then $MN = 10 - x$. Substitute these expressions in the given equation: $x = \frac{1}{3}(10 - x)$

Solve for x: $x = \frac{10}{3} - \frac{x}{3} \rightarrow x + \frac{x}{3} = \frac{10}{3} \rightarrow \frac{4x}{3} = \frac{10}{3} \rightarrow 4x = 10 \rightarrow x = \frac{10}{4} = \frac{5}{2} = 2.5$

$x = OM$. Point O is at -6. Then, point M is at: $-6 + 2.5 = -3.5$

20) Choice C is correct

First, calculate Jack's riding time in minutes: 1 hour 20 minutes = 80 minutes

Then, convert kilometers to meters: 160 kilometers = 160,000 meters

Now simplify the ratio to find the answer: $\frac{160,000}{80} = 2,000$ meters

21) Choice D is correct

If x is the smaller consecutive integer, then $x + 1$ is the larger consecutive integer. Use their sum (-13) to find x: $x + (x + 1) = -13 \rightarrow 2x + 1 = -13 \rightarrow 2x = -14 \rightarrow x = -7$

The two consecutive integers are -7 and -6. 2 is added to the smaller integer: $-7 + 2 = -5$, and 3 is subtracted from the larger integer: $-6 - 3 = -9$ find the product: $-5 \times (-9) = 45$

22) Choice D is Correct

The capacity of a red box is 20% bigger than the capacity of a blue box and it can hold 30 books. Therefore, we want to find a number that 20% bigger than that number is 30. Let x be that number. Then: $1.20 \times x = 30$. Divide both sides of the equation by 1.2. Then: $x = \frac{30}{1.20} = 25$

23) Choice D is Correct

Use FOIL method. $(2x + y)(x - 2y) = 2x^2 - 4xy + xy - 2y^2 = 2x^2 - 2y^2 - 3xy$

24) Choice B is correct

The equation of a line in slope intercept form is: $y = mx + b$. Solve for y.

$4x - 2y = 12 \Rightarrow -2y = 12 - 4x \Rightarrow y = (12 - 4x) \div (-2) \Rightarrow y = 2x - 6$. The slope of this line is 2. The product of the slopes of two perpendicular lines is -1. Therefore, the slope of a line that is perpendicular to this line is: $m_1 \times m_2 = -1 \Rightarrow 2 \times m_2 = -1 \Rightarrow m_2 = \frac{-1}{2} = -\frac{1}{2}$

25) Choice C is correct

Convert everything into an equation: $35 = (3 \times \text{shirt}) - 10$

Now, solve the equation: $45 = 3 \text{ shirt} \rightarrow \text{shirt} = \frac{45}{3} = 15$. The price of the shirt was \$15.

26) Choice D is correct

First, convert the improper fraction to a mixed number: $-\frac{32}{5} = -6\frac{2}{5}$

The two closest integers to this fraction are -7 and -6. The integer less than $-\frac{32}{5}$ is -7.

27) Choice D is correct

Let x equal the smallest angle of the triangle. Then, the three angles are $x, 3x$, and $5x$. The sum of the angles of a triangle is 180. Set up an equation using this to find x:

$x + 3x + 5x = 180 \rightarrow 9x = 180 \rightarrow x = 20$

Since the question asks for the measure of the largest angle, $5x = 5(20) = 100°$

28) Choice D is correct

The angle $(2x - 5)$ and 55 are supplementary angles. Therefore:

$(2x - 5) + 55 = 180 \rightarrow 2x + 50 = 180 \rightarrow 2x = 180 - 50 = 130 \rightarrow x = \frac{130}{2} \rightarrow x = 65$

PERT Mathematics Practice Tests Answers and Explanations

29) Choice B is correct

Divide 40 by 4: $\dfrac{\left(\dfrac{40(x+1)}{4}\right)-10}{12} \to \dfrac{10(x+1)-10}{12}$. Distribute 10 through the parentheses $(x+1)$

$\dfrac{10x+10-10}{12} = \dfrac{10x}{12} = \dfrac{5}{6}x$

30) Choice C is correct

Area of the circle is $144\pi\ ft^2$. Use the formula of area of the circle to find the radius.

Area of the circle $= \pi r^2 \Rightarrow 144\pi = \pi r^2 \Rightarrow 144 = r^2 \Rightarrow r = 12$

Radius of the circle is equal than $12\ ft$. Therefore, the diameter of the circle is twice of the radius. So, the diameter is $24\ ft$.

PERT Mathematics Practice Test 2

Answers and Explanations

1) Choice D is correct

The equation of a line is in the form of $y = mx + b$, where m is the slope of the line and b is the $y-$intercept of the line. Two points $(1,2)$ and $(-1,6)$ are on line A. Therefore, the slope of the line A is: $m = \frac{y_2 - y_1}{x_2 - x_1} = \frac{6-2}{-1-1} = \frac{4}{-2} = -2$

The slope of line A is -2. Thus, the formula of the line A is: $y = -2x + b$, choose a point and plug in the values of x and y in the equation to solve for b. Let's choose point $(1, 2)$. Then:

$y = -2x + b \to 2 = -2(1) + b \to b = 2 + 2 = 4$

The equation of line A is: $y = -2x + 4$. So, only point $(3, -2)$ could be on the line.

2) Choice C is correct

Divide 4 by $\frac{1}{3}$: $4 \div \frac{1}{3} = 4 \times 3 = 12$

3) Choice B is correct

$2m = n + 5 \to m = \frac{n+5}{2}$. Substitute each value of n to find the values of m:

$m = \frac{5+5}{2} = \frac{10}{2} = 5$

$m = \frac{3+5}{2} = \frac{8}{2} = 4$

$m = \frac{7+5}{2} = \frac{12}{2} = 6$

The set of m is $\{5,4,6\}$

4) Choice A is correct

Apply the distributive property; multiply the -2 by $2x$ and 1. Then combine like terms:

$7x + 3 - 2(2x + 1) = 13 \to 7x + 3 - 4x - 2 = 13 \to 3x + 1 = 13 \to 3x = 12$

Divide both sides of the equation by 3: $x = 4$

5) Choice B is correct

Plug in 25 for x in the equation.

A. $\quad x + 10 = 40 \to 25 + 10 \neq 40$

B. $\quad 4x = 100 \to 4(25) = 100$

C. $\quad 3x = 70 \to 3(25) \neq 70$

D. $\quad \frac{x}{2} = 12 \to \frac{25}{2} \neq 12$

Only choice B is correct.

6) Choice D is correct

Jack scored a mean of 80 per test. In the first 4 tests, the sum of scores is: $80 \times 4 = 320$. Now, calculate the mean over the 5 tests: $\frac{320+90}{5} = \frac{410}{5} = 82$

7) Choice A is correct

Volume of the cube is less than $64 \; m^3$. Use the formula of volume of cubes.

Volume $= (one\; side)^3 \Rightarrow 64 = (one\; side)^3$. Find the cube root of both sides.

$64 = (one\; side)^3 \to one\; side = \sqrt[3]{64} = 4$

Then: $4 =$ one side. The side of the cube is less than 4. Only choice A is less than 4.

8) Choice C is correct

Simplify and combine like terms.

$(5x^3 - 8x^2 + 2x^4) - (4x^2 - 2x^4 + 2x^3) \Rightarrow 5x^3 - 8x^2 + 2x^4 - 4x^2 + 2x^4 - 2x^3 \Rightarrow$
$4x^4 + 3x^3 - 12x^2$

9) Choice B is correct

The sum of all the internal angles of a simple polygon is $180(n-2)$ where n is the number of sides, so $180(4-2) = 180 \times 2 = 360$. Vertical angles are congruent. Then:

$\to 360 = 120 + 120 + 98 + c \to c = 360 - 338 = 22$

10) Choice D is correct

Let's review the choices when $x = 1$

A. $f(x) = x^2 - 5 \quad$ if $x = 1 \to f(1) = (1)^2 - 5 = 1 - 5 = -4 \neq 5$

B. $f(x) = x^2 - 1 \quad$ if $x = 1 \to f(1) = (1)^2 - 1 = 1 - 1 = 0 \neq 5$

C. $f(x) = \sqrt{x + 2} \quad$ if $x = 1 \to f(1) = \sqrt{1 + 2} = \sqrt{3} \neq 5$

D. $f(x) = \sqrt{x} + 4 \quad$ if $x = 1 \to f(1) = \sqrt{1} + 4 = 5$

Only choice D provides a correct answer.

11) **Choice C is correct**

First draw an isosceles triangle. Remember that two legs of the triangle are equal.

Let put a for the legs. Then:

$a = 6 \Rightarrow$ Area of the triangle is $= \frac{1}{2}(6 \times 6) = \frac{36}{2} = 18 \ cm^2$

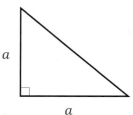

12) **Choice C is correct**

Solve for x: $0.00104 = \frac{104}{x}$, multiply both sides by x, $(0.00104)(x) = \frac{104}{x}(x)$.

Simplify: $0.00104x = 104$. Divide both side by 0.00104: $\frac{0.00104x}{0.00104} = \frac{104}{0.00104}$, simplify:

$x = \dfrac{104}{0.00104} = 100{,}000$

13) **Choice D is correct**

The number of cards in the bag is 15. Probability $= \dfrac{number\ of\ desired\ outcomes}{number\ of\ total\ outcomes} = \dfrac{1}{15}$

14) **Choice B is correct**

$(2x + 4)°$ and $96°$ are vertical angles. Vertical angles are equal in measure. Then:

$2x + 4 = 96 \rightarrow 2x = 92 \rightarrow x = 46°$

15) **Choice B is correct**

First calculate square of -3: $|-5| + 9 \times 2\frac{1}{3} + 9$

Convert mix number to fraction, then multiply to 9: $|-5| + \frac{63}{3} + 9$

Calculate absolute value and add terms: $5 + 21 + 9 = 35$

16) **Choice B is correct**

The two-digit numbers must be even, so the only possible two-digit numbers must end in 6, since 6 is the only even digit given in the problem. Since the numbers cannot be repeated, the only possibilities for two-digit even numbers are 76 and 56. Thus, the answer is two possible two-digit numbers.

PERT Mathematics Practice Tests Answers and Explanations

17) Choice A is correct

First convert 24 inches to feet. 12 inch $= 1$ feet, thus: $24 \div 12 = 2$ feet. Then, calculate the volume, in cubic feet: $25 \times 6 \times 2 = 300$

18) Choice C is correct

Use properties of equations to determine the missing expression. $\frac{2y}{x} - \frac{y}{3x} = \frac{(\ldots)}{3x}$

$\frac{3}{3} \cdot \frac{2y}{x} - \frac{y}{3x} = \frac{(\ldots)}{3x} \to \frac{6y}{3x} - \frac{y}{3x} = \frac{(\ldots)}{3x} \to \frac{6y - y}{3x} = \frac{(\ldots)}{3x} \to (\ldots) = 5y$

19) Choice C is correct

Since 90 boxes contain 360 kg vegetable. Therefore, 1 box contains $\frac{360 \, kg}{90} = 4 \, kg$ vegetable.

20) Choice C is correct

Let n represent a number in the sequence, and let x represent the number that comes just before n.

$n = 4 + 2x \to 84 = 4 + 2x \to 80 = 2x \to x = 40$

21) Choice D is correct

$\frac{38}{50} = 0.76$, converting 0.76 to percent we have: $0.76 = 76\%$. Then, 38 is 76% of 50.

22) Choice A is correct

Perimeter of rectangle is equal to the sum of all the sides of the rectangle:

Perimeter $= 2(14) + 2(5) = 28 + 10 = 38 \, cm$

23) Choice D is correct

To solve absolute values equations, write two equations. $x - 10$ could be positive 3, or negative 3. Therefore, $x - 10 = 3 \Rightarrow x = 13$

$x - 10 = -3 \Rightarrow x = 7$. Find the product of the solutions: $7 \times 13 = 91$

24) Choice D is correct

$3\frac{1}{4} + 2\frac{4}{16} + 1\frac{3}{8} + 5\frac{1}{2}$

Convert all the fractions to a common denominator (16):

$3\frac{4}{16} + 2\frac{4}{16} + 1\frac{6}{16} + 5\frac{8}{16} = (3 + 2 + 1 + 5) + \left(\frac{4+4+6+8}{16}\right) = 11 + 1\frac{6}{16} = 12\frac{6}{16} = 12\frac{3}{8}$

25) Choice B is correct

One gram is equal to 1,000 milligrams, or 1 milligram is equal to $\frac{1}{1,000}$ gram

Thus, 85 milligrams $= \frac{85}{1,000} = 0.085$ gram

26) Choice B is correct

Substitute 6 for m and -3 for n:

$$\frac{5 - 9(3 + n)}{3m - 5(2 - n)} = \frac{5 - 9(3 + (-3))}{3(6) - 5(2 - (-3))} = \frac{5 - 9(0)}{18 - 5(5)} = \frac{5}{18 - 25} = \frac{5}{-7} = -\frac{5}{7}$$

27) Choice B is correct

To answer this question, we need to divide 28 by 7: $\frac{28}{7} = 4$

28) Choice B is correct

Simple interest (y) is calculated by multiplying the initial deposit (p), by the interest rate (r), and time (t). $360 = 240 \times 0.10 \times t \to 360 = 24t \to t = \frac{360}{24} = 15$

So, it takes 15 years to get $360 with an investment of $240.

29) Choice C is correct

There are 60 minutes in 1 hours. Divide the number of minutes by the number of minutes in 1 hour: $\frac{1,800}{60} = 30$ hours

30) Choice A is correct

First, find the sale price. 15% of $45.00 is $6.75, so the sale price is $45.00 - $6.75 = $38.25. Next, find the price after Nick's employee discount. 20% × $38.25 = $7.65, so, the final price of the shoes is $38.25 - $7.65 = $30.60.

Effortless Math's PERT Online Center

... So Much More Online!

Effortless Math Online PERT Math Center offers a complete study program, including the following:

- ✓ Step-by-step instructions on how to prepare for the PERT Math test
- ✓ Numerous PERT Math worksheets to help you measure your math skills
- ✓ Complete list of PERT Math formulas
- ✓ Video lessons for PERT Math topics
- ✓ Full-length PERT Math practice tests
- ✓ And much more…

No Registration Required.

Visit **EffortlessMath.com/PERT** to find your online PERT Math resources.

Receive the PDF version of this book or get another FREE book!

Thank you for using our Book!

Do you LOVE this book?

Then, you can get the PDF version of this book or another book absolutely FREE!

Please email us at:

info@EffortlessMath.com

for details.

Author's Final Note

I hope you enjoyed reading this book. You've made it through the book! Great job!

First of all, thank you for purchasing this practice book. I know you could have picked any number of books to help you prepare for your PERT Math test, but you picked this book and for that I am extremely grateful.

It took me years to write this workbook for the PERT Math because I wanted to prepare a comprehensive PERT Math workbook to help test takers make the most effective use of their valuable time while preparing for the test.

After teaching and tutoring math courses for over a decade, I've gathered my personal notes and lessons to develop this practice book. It is my greatest hope that the exercises in this book could help you prepare for your test successfully.

If you have any questions, please contact me at reza@effortlessmath.com and I will be glad to assist. Your feedback will help me to greatly improve the quality of my books in the future and make this book even better. Furthermore, I expect that I have made a few minor errors somewhere in this book. If you think this to be the case, please let me know so I can fix the issue as soon as possible.

If you enjoyed this book and found some benefit in reading this, I'd like to hear from you and hope that you could take a quick minute to post a review on the book's Amazon page. To leave your valuable feedback, please visit: amzn.to/2NFZGJy

Or scan this QR code.

I personally go over every single review, to make sure my books really are reaching out and helping students and test takers. Please help me help PERT Math test takers, by leaving a review!

I wish you all the best in your future success!

Reza Nazari
Math teacher and author

Made in United States
Orlando, FL
07 July 2022